THE FORGIVENESS WAY

A 40-Day Prayer Devotional on Letting Go and Moving Forward

MICAH E. DAVIS

TYNDALE MOMENTUM®

A Tyndale nonfiction imprint

Visit Tyndale online at tyndale.com.

Visit Tyndale Momentum online at tyndalemomentum.com.

Visit the author online at micahedavis.com.

Tyndale, Tyndale's quill logo, *Tyndale Momentum*, and the Tyndale Momentum logo are registered trademarks of Tyndale House Ministries, registered in the United States of America. Tyndale Momentum is a nonfiction imprint of Tyndale House Publishers, Carol Stream, Illinois.

The Forgiveness Way: A 40-Day Prayer Devotional on Letting Go and Moving Forward

Cover design by Dean Renninger

Interior design by Brandi Davis

Edited by Claire Lloyd

Published in association with the literary agency of The Steve Laube Agency.

For information about special discounts for bulk purchases, please contact Tyndale House Publishers at csresponse@tyndale.com, or call 1-855-277-9400.

ISBN 979-8-4005-0144-9

Printed in China

32 31 30 29 28 27 26
7 6 5 4 3 2 1

To Rylei,

As I promised you the day I married you: I vow to build a life with you upon the foundation of consistency, faithfulness, blood, sweat, tears, **forgiveness, forgiveness again***, kindness, tenderness, and patience.*

I love you.

CONTENTS

Prologue

PROCEED WITH CAUTION

Every day after basketball practice in college, I would slowly make my way to the athletic trainer's room where a giant, swirling pool awaited. From the outside, you might imagine it to be a relaxing hot tub that would bring relief and relaxation. But as you ventured closer, you would see the sign: "Cold Water Immersion Tub: Proceed with Caution."

This sign emphatically clarified that what was ahead would not be relaxing or enjoyable. However, as time went on, I found post-practice ice baths to be a necessity.

Basketball is a physical sport. At its highest level, you are competing with athletes who require you to match their full exertion of energy over and over and over again. Practicing with twelve physically primed men involved running, jumping, and swinging at full speed for two hours on a daily basis, which left many of us bruised and battered. The training room was where recovery took place.

The initial plunge was a sensation I never got used to or looked forward to. But I knew that it was necessary to experience the healing I longed for. Over time, I found that the cold water immersion tub was a healing agent. The bumps and bruises I accrued on a daily basis felt much better after fifteen to twenty minutes in the ice bath. The cold water soon became a tranquil oasis.

Life is also a physical sport requiring recovery. You are competing with people of all shapes, sizes, backgrounds, and giftings for meaning, purpose, and recognition. At least, that's what life wants you to think. The rat race of life convinces us that we must scrap, claw, and fight for what we think we deserve. In the midst of that pursuit of happiness, many of us end up bruised and battered in the process.

But there is a way forward.

A way that heals.

And it is the way of forgiveness.

If you struggle to forgive, you aren't alone. In the last two decades of my life, I've had to work through the process of forgiving as I've watched father figure after father figure fail. I've felt hurt, betrayed, and abandoned.

And yet . . .

I have witnessed God—the great healer—show up time after time. Out of the pain has come healing—and forgiveness. I share more about this journey in *Three Strikes, You're Forgiven: Encounter a God Who Wants to Redeem Your Past, Restore Your Present, and Transform Your Future*, and out of that work has come this one. A forty-day journey exploring the process of forgiveness, reconciliation, and redemption.

And so, here we are. For whatever reason, you've decided to pick up this prayer book on forgiveness. My guess is, it's because you're searching and longing for anything that may offer healing to the pain inside your soul.

Friend, you are immensely brave for taking the plunge into the icy waters. And though we may not know each other well, before that initial sensation convinces you to jump out, I would invite you to trust the words my trainer told me: "This is safe. You're okay. This is what's best for you. This is how healing takes place."

Let the cold tub become an oasis for your soul. It may be uncomfortable, but it is not unbearable.

The Catholic writer Ron Rolheiser notes, "Before we die, we need to forgive. We need to forgive those who hurt us, to forgive ourselves for not being any better than those who hurt us, to forgive life itself for some of the things that it dealt us, and, not least, to forgive God for the fact that life is unfair, so as not to die with a bitter and angry heart."[1]

The way forward is forgiveness.

To forgive others.

To ask for forgiveness.

To forgive ourselves.

And to forgive God himself.

It's far easier said than done, but it is possible when we look to the cross.

Jesus can transform our wounds into scars. This process reminds me of the beautiful art form known as *kintsugi*.

The origins of *kintsugi* art are unknown, but legend has it that in the late fifteenth century a shogun named Ashikaga Yoshimasa sent a damaged Chinese tea bowl back to China to be fixed.[2] The returned item was an aesthetic disaster, and—seeking to innovate—the craftsmen began to tinker with broken ceramics in an effort to repair damaged products.

Eventually the craftsmen developed the art form of *kintsugi*. Taking broken ceramics, they would carefully, delicately mend these fractured pieces back together with hints of gold. Over time, their intent moved away from restoring these pieces to their original state. Instead, the artisans began purposefully highlighting the damaged areas—"scars," as they've come to be known.[3]

Do you see where I'm going with this?

Kintsugi art is a beautiful representation of the journey of forgiveness. Inevitably we wound and hurt others and are in turn wounded and hurt by them, shattering relationships and trust. Yet as we mature in Christ, as we encounter the weight of our sins and also the depth of his grace, we are healed. We are mended. We are restored. We are forgiven. And in that, we are afforded the ability to forgive.

My friends, our lives all have potential to be *kintsugi* art pieces. They tell a story, not of perfection but of redemption. Our lives show others how—through Jesus—beauty is possible in brokenness. How devotion can develop out of despair. How pain can be transformed into purpose.

Your *kintsugi* piece isn't finished yet. In fact, it's just getting started.

God wants to use you, every part of you—your flaws, hurts, wounds, pain—to change this world as we know it. To help bring heaven on earth.

So how do we begin the process of forgiveness? It starts with an invitation—and the invitation is a simple one each day. Forgive.

Forgive those who abandoned you when you needed them. Forgive yourself for the anger you can't seem to let go of. Forgive the person you will one day be who makes mistakes of their own. Remember, I said it was simple, not easy. But the opportunity before us is massive.

In a world of cynicism, we have an opportunity to prophetically witness to those around us regarding what people of compassion are like. In a world that focuses on failure, we can reenvision the power of reconciliation.

It's going to require bravery and courage to come afresh to these pages each day, to meditate on these words as if they are a mirror reflecting the brokenness in our own lives, not a microscope to focus on the failings of others. It will take courage to pray fervently for Jesus to heal the fractured pieces of your life. Your hurt is valid. Your pain is real.

But we serve a God who wants to redeem all the past hurts you've endured, restore your present self with the dignity and value you inherently carry, and transform your future into one that breaks generational chains of bitterness and resentment.

Healing is possible. It's going to require some grit to absorb the initial shock and discomfort of the icy waters we're sinking into. But on the other side? On the other side is the life you've always longed for. A life of freedom, peace, and love.

So, let's dip our toes in, together. My hope and prayer is that over time we trust Jesus—the Wounded Healer himself—enough to fully immerse ourselves in the beautiful but backward way of living that he offers.

The way of forgiveness.

PART I

Forgiving Others

Day 1

FAMILY MATTERS

Azor the father of Zadok, Zadok the father of Akim, Akim the father of Elihud, Elihud the father of Eleazar, Eleazar the father of Matthan, Matthan the father of Jacob, and Jacob the father of Joseph, the husband of Mary, and Mary was the mother of Jesus who is called the Messiah.

MATTHEW 1:14-16

Options. So many options.

We have enough choices to make nowadays that we've even labeled the phenomenon of our modern moment. When choice becomes overwhelming, it can be called choice anxiety.

But there is one choice that none of us get to make. And that is our family of origin.

For some, our family of origin elicits feelings of immense gratitude or joy. For others, in a world full of divorce, separation, and relational strife, our family of origin has brought more pain and heartache than perhaps any other facet of life.

You did not choose the mother who gave birth to you. The mother whose struggles you and your siblings may have watched firsthand as young children. The mother who was stronger than you knew.

You did not choose your father. The father who may have spent more time at the office than in the backyard. The father who worked too hard to provide.

Perhaps there were too many milestone moments when Mom or Dad (or both) weren't there. Or perhaps they did show up for you, imperfect but present.

Maybe you had to grow up far too early. You became the man or woman of the house and had to protect others when you needed protection. You had to provide and put food on the table when that should have been provided for you. Or maybe you were overly protected, unable to learn and grow in the ways that you needed to despite your parents' best intentions.

Your childhood may have been a dream. If that's the case, I encourage you to pause and pray a prayer of gratitude! Family who cares for one another well is a blessing. That is—unfortunately—not the norm.

For many of us, the family we didn't choose is a source of pain, and in some cases, the difficulty is exasperated by the proximity we maintain.

The parents who drink too much host extended holidays.

The sibling who is argumentative still lives nearby.

The aunt who disapproves of your spouse is always at that annual family get-together.

The proximity (or lack thereof) might be a constant reminder of these family dynamics.

I can't pretend to know why you were born into the family you were. But there is Someone who does. And he wastes nothing. The invitation before you is to trust in a God who can use all things for good.

Easier said than done? Sure.

But nonetheless necessary. Pain that is not transformed is transferred. Right now, your relationships are being affected. You may not realize it, but you may even be establishing similar relational patterns that will only continue the generational cycle that you are a by-product of.

However, that can change. Today.

But not all at once.

This is a slow process. We're only at the beginning of our journey. This may be a prayer you need to return to, day after day, for weeks or months, if not years.

You did not choose the family you were born into. But you can choose to chart a new course, to go a different direction. To recognize what was of value and what you don't want to repeat.

That way is a difficult route to traverse. But on the other side is the freedom, joy, and contentment that you've been longing for.

Every day of this forty-day journey together, I'd like to invite you to take action through prayer. I hold firmly to the conviction that prayer changes things. And so, I encourage you to invite Jesus into the dark spaces of your life. To let the Prince of Peace reign where anxiety has ruled. To speak words of life into places of lament.

So, my friend, I encourage you to make the choice.

Choose forgiveness.

Choose redemption.

Choose to love the family you did not choose.

Prayer

Jesus,

I did not choose the family I was born into, but you did.

Why? I hope, in time, you will reveal that to me.

Until then, I'm asking that you heal the past hurts that I cannot understand and give me grace to see the ways that my family did show up for me.

The ways that they let me down, I offer to you.

Thank you that I can learn from my family of origin which choices I do or don't want to repeat.

To write a new story in my own life, I know that I must make a different choice. For the ways I've been burdened or blessed by my family . . .

I choose to believe that you, God, are near.

I choose to believe that you, God, are just.

I choose to believe that you, God, hold truth.

I choose to believe that you, God, can heal.

God, you invite me into your family when I trust in you.

You instruct us to call you "Father."

I trust there is intentionality behind that vernacular.

You are the perfect parent.

You hold me where I've been dropped. You protect me where I've been exposed. You fight for me where I've been forgotten.

Help me to become more and more like you—full of joy, peace, and love.

If I'm tempted to focus on flaws, help me to pursue reconciliation.

If I'm tempted to repeat generational patterns, help me to pursue healing.

If I'm tempted to put my family on a pedestal, help me to put you first.

Help me to love and forgive the family I did not choose as you love and forgive me.

Amen.

Day 2

TRAINING WHEELS

Speak and act as those who are going to be judged by the law that gives freedom, because judgment without mercy will be shown to anyone who has not been merciful. **Mercy triumphs over judgment.**

JAMES 2:12-13, emphasis mine

The curb was cracked. It was roughly four inches high, rounded, and in rough shape. It seemed primed for my bicycle tire to hit it at just the right angle to send me over my handlebars.

At three years old, this was my first ride without training wheels, and my dad told me I was ready. He told me he would be right there to catch me if I stumbled. But I had caught on quicker than he thought, so he let me go.

Then came the curb. And a crash. And pain.

The crash itself hurt enough, but I didn't realize at first the subtle messaging that had been embedded into me that day. I came to subconsciously believe *I'm not safe. Danger and risk should be avoided.*

That was a long time ago, but to my dismay, I am often more like that younger version of myself than I like to admit. Rather than getting up right after a fall, I'm often tempted to take the easier route and avoid the risks God might be calling me to. That's what pain does. It creates deeper layers within you that take far longer to heal than the initial event.

Like hitting a curb, forgiveness can be painful.

Perhaps the most difficult aspect of forgiveness is that there's no formula to it. If there were a step 1-2-3 process, you wouldn't be reading this. We'd all be experts.

But forgiveness is more complicated than that, isn't it?

It's less of a formula and more of a fire. It's messy, uncomfortable, and almost never linear. Typically, forgiveness involves taking three steps forward and two steps back. There are good days, and there are hard days. However, as I heard John Mark Comer say at a retreat, "You can either allow the fire of life to burn you out or to burn you clean."[1]

The hurt we accrue over the course of time becomes like bruises. They're hardly noticeable until they're poked or prodded. And then the pain is incessant . . . until they're healed. The only way to get rid of a bruise is to give it time. Momentary pain in exchange for genuine healing.

See, it's true. It is less painful to avoid forgiveness than to go into the fire. Like riding a bike with training wheels, there's minimal risk involved if we play it safe in our relationships. But there's so much that is missed out on in the long run. And the pain of relational conflict later on will far outweigh the few bumps and bruises accrued in learning how to forgive.

So, take off the proverbial training wheels. Allow God to meet you in your pain. Feel the burn. Because the fire is a crucible that has the potential to burn you clean.

Prayer

Lord,

I would like to spend a few moments recalling times that I've seen your faithfulness.

I invite you into these moments.

You already know that I've experienced pain in my past . . .

I invite you into these moments, too, Jesus.

Help me to acknowledge your guiding hand in both.

Allow me to recall the deeper messages that were embedded into my body and soul from these experiences.

Separate the truth from the lies.

Dignify my experience but also detangle my feelings of hurt or remorse.

Father, I understand that this journey of forgiveness is like entering a crucible. It is not for the faint of heart.

But I deeply desire healing. And I know that can only come through the fire of forgiveness.

Grant me the courage that forgiveness requires. It is a fundamental loss to incur, a debt that you're asking me to offer free credit toward—in exchange for freedom.

You are not asking me to do anything for anyone that you have not first done for me.

So, help me get to a place where I believe and trust that mercy triumphs over judgment.

Refine me in the fire, Lord Jesus. I long to become like you.

I know the first step toward forgiving is where I must begin to become perfect, as you—heavenly Father—are perfect.

Amen.

Day 3

SIBLING RIVALRY

The LORD said to Cain, "Why are you angry? Why is your face downcast? If you do what is right, will you not be accepted? But if you do not do what is right, sin is crouching at your door; it desires to have you, but you must rule over it."

GENESIS 4:6-7

Watch this! Watch this! Watch this!

No, watch THIS!

Any parent can envision this scenario. Two siblings fighting for your attention as they show off their newest-learned skill. But for many of us, our children's actions can bring up our own painful memories of being overshadowed, overlooked, or seemingly forgotten.

Whether you have siblings or not, we've all vied for someone else's attention. Usually, this attention-seeking includes competition.

The fight to be noticed by your boss over other coworkers for a promotion.

The struggle to find a spouse or have children when it appears that everyone else has already started family life.

The pain of comparing your life to other people's and feeling that you come up short.

If we're honest, the pain of such rejection—whether from others or ourselves—can leave a searing mark on our soul. And in the midst of this, we are offered a choice.

In Genesis 4, Cain and Abel bring forth offerings to the Lord. Cain offers the firstfruits of the soil, and Abel offers fat portions from some of the firstborn of his flock.[1] Two brothers vying for their father's attention. The Scriptures note that the Lord looked with favor on Abel and his offering but did not on Cain and his offering. Why? Hebrews 11:4 says, "By faith Abel brought God a better offering than Cain did."

So, in what surely felt like rejection, Cain had a choice to make: He could choose to believe the best or the worst about God. And God seems to be ahead of Cain in clarifying this. He asks Cain, "Why are you angry? Why is your face downcast? If you do what is right, will you not be accepted? But if you do not do what is right, sin is crouching at your door; it desires to have you, but you must rule over it."

There are moments in life when—for whatever reason—we seemingly receive the short end of the stick. This can occur justifiably or unjustifiably. Either way, rejection is a part of life. The question before you and me is this: How will we respond when we feel like we've *lost*?

When she gets the promotion over you?

When your church community doesn't treat singleness as a gift?

When they get pregnant on the first try?

God tells Cain that if he does what is right, he will be accepted. But God doesn't say that Cain will be rewarded, favored, successful, or picked first. Sometimes, we are overlooked—never by our heavenly Father, but certainly by our earthly families, our employers, and our heroes.

As you reflect on the moments throughout your life when you've faced rejection, how have you responded? Cain makes the fateful mistake of responding in anger and bitterness. His contempt for his brother is rooted in pride—Cain is convinced that he deserves the praise Abel is getting.

Often, those decisions aren't up to us. When we do receive the praise, the attention, or the credit, we should graciously and humbly receive it. But when our efforts aren't acknowledged? We should continue to choose what is right, knowing that we are accepted by a heavenly Father who loves and sees what others do not.

Those who idolize the attention of others can end up desperate enough to kill for it—as Cain did. Those who forgive the people who have overlooked them experience a peace and joy that can only be found in the secure identity of a son or daughter who has full trust in their Father.

Give your offering faithfully; trust that if you do what is right, you will be accepted; and let forgiveness—not bitterness—wash over your soul.

Prayer

Adonai,

You know what it is like to be outright rejected.

Often I feel that I have done the right thing but have been unjustifiably overlooked.

Jesus, would you please bring these instances to the surface of my soul now, and—one by one—would you help to extend forgiveness to anyone I am holding resentment toward?

God, I confess that I have also done the right thing with the wrong motive in my heart. I must ask for forgiveness for the ways that I have allowed pride to transform into bitterness when I have not received what I believe I deserve. I know that you give good gifts and bless us beyond what we deserve.

Even when I'm not, you are faithful.

Even when I don't believe, you hold me securely.

Even when I reject you, you love me.

Jesus, there is no one who understands rejection more than you.

Yet, even as you experienced rejection, you offered forgiveness.

So today help me to do the same.

Help me to forgive the individuals who seemed to forget me.

Help me to notice the ways that sin—and its trap of bitterness and cynicism—is crouching at the door of my heart.

Help me instead to pursue reconciliation, secure in my identity in you.

Amen.

Day 4

CALLED BY NAME

When Jesus reached the spot, he looked up and said to him, "Zacchaeus, come down immediately. I must stay at your house today."

LUKE 19:5

Throughout the New Testament, we see Jesus gathering sinners, saints, and skeptics alike around tables to partake in meals together. There is undeniable beauty to life around a table. We are relational beings. As Dr. Todd Hall notes, "We are loved into loving."[1] The table is a central element to this truth being realized.

However, for many, the table—especially a table within a community, such as a workplace or church—can be a source of pain.

At the table, exclusion occurs.

At the table, gossip happens.

At the table, people are ignored.

Do any of the above describe an experience you've had?

One early instance burned into my memory is from the fifth-grade school lunchroom, where I was sarcastically dubbed "Freak Out

Micah!" in response to a passionate defense I gave for my Christian faith.

As the cafeteria quieted and I felt the stares, I wanted to run and hide and never return. The internal script that developed from my experience blunted the passion I had, not just for Jesus but for all sorts of things in my life for years. The lie that I began to believe was that I should hold no strong convictions. I never wanted to be typecast as too over-the-top.

In Luke 19, we witness a tax collector named Zacchaeus encounter Jesus. Nowadays we are mostly unable to comprehend the hate, disgust, and vitriol that was directed toward tax collectors in Jesus' time. These were ethnic Jews who had sold out to Rome as workers in order to make large sums of money. They were willing to turn against and exploit their own people for personal gain.

How many times a day do you think Zacchaeus was called by his name? Perhaps he was more affectionally known as "Pig! Swine! No-good, dirty, rotten tax collector!"

But notice how Jesus talks to this man: "When Jesus reached the spot, he looked up and said to him, 'Zacchaeus, come down immediately. I must stay at your house today.'"

Jesus addresses Zacchaeus by name. And then he invites him to the table. At the table, Zacchaeus finds salvation—healing!

What about you?

For those of us who have felt unwelcome at the table, Jesus says, "Come home. I must dine with you today."

For those of us who have been excluded, Jesus restores to us an identity that is secure.

For those who have been slandered, Jesus calls you by your name.

For those who have been lied about, Jesus speaks truth into your soul.

For those of us who have been broken, cast out, or damaged, Jesus says, "Salvation—healing, wholeness—is available to you."

But for those of us who have been unwilling to welcome others to the table, we are given this story as a challenge regarding what it means to seek and save the lost.

Our Savior is a God who redeems, even at the table.

Prayer

Abba Father,

You see me.

You see me at my workplace. You see me packing my lunch and running out the door. You see me sitting alone at the break room table.

You see me when I am chastised, forgotten, or gossiped about.

You see me. And you call me by name.

My name.

Holy Spirit, help me during these painful moments, and give me the strength to forgive—by name—the people in my community who haven't welcomed me. Let me be someone who invites others to the table.

Jesus, thank you for being Lord of the table. Where I've experienced past pain, I ask that you would give me new experiences—full of laughter, friends, good food, and great wine.

You are a God who feasts. And to the table, you invite me, just as I am.

Amen.

Day 5

THE PLACE OF HONOR

They replied, "Let one of us sit at your right and the other at your left in your glory."

MARK 10:37

No one likes being left out.

My anxiety heightens to abnormal levels when I round a corner into a room where people are talking and—upon my arrival—stop.

Is it me?

Did I do something?

What are they talking about?

Over time, if I'm not careful, cynicism can begin to infect my entire perspective toward relationships. Maybe for you too.

"Why even try? It's not worth the effort," we say.

Being excluded hurts. Why? If I'm honest, for me, it's usually because of my ego. Exclusion can be a painful reminder that someone else is seen, wanted, or desired and I am not.

Now, I don't believe this innate desire to feel seen, valued, and worthy is inherently a bad thing. The problem is, we can over-inflate that desire to a level of pride. Beneath the surface of pride is entitlement—the belief that we deserve to be included in all things by all people at all times. But Jesus rebukes this thinking.

In Mark 10, James and John ask to be given the most exclusive seats of honor in heaven, to sit at the right and left of Jesus. Understandably, the other disciples become indignant (probably because *they* want those seats). And how does Jesus respond? "You know that those who are regarded as rulers of the Gentiles lord it over them, and their high officials exercise authority over them. Not so with you. Instead, whoever wants to become great among you must be your servant, and whoever wants to be first must be slave of all."[1]

In other words, everyone wants to be included and seen as important. Not so with you. Jesus asks you to instead seek the places of lowest honor. Don't worry about being seen; worry about being a servant.

This is a countercultural attitude, but I think it helps us to unwind much of the hurt we feel in being left out. Please hear me: Your pain is real. And the times you've been excluded were probably unfair, petty, or just plain mean. But these moments are also opportunities to grow in Christlikeness.

The fact of the matter is that you and I do not deserve to be included in eternity. But—through Jesus—we are. He welcomes us into his family as a son or daughter, an heir to God's Kingdom.

Think about that.

Where have you been included throughout your life: your friend group, the break room, the church pew, or the cubicle? In the same way, God sees you and says, "You. I choose you."

So, today, an invitation lies before us to forgive the times we've been left out and to remember our true identity. God has included you. God has chosen you. Where you were relationally rejected, God has relationally purchased you with the precious blood of Jesus.

My friend, that is enough. And if we find our enough in Jesus, then we may just be able to muster up the courage to forgive.

Prayer

Father,

If I am honest, I have prioritized being included by others more than I have graciously acknowledged being included by you.

You did not have to send your Son to die for me.

You did not have to choose me.

You did not have to include me.

But you did!

So, Jesus, would you help me to believe that is enough today?

Would you bring to mind a recent moment when I have been excluded?

And as I recall this moment, would you remind me of my identity in you?

I am not forgotten, excluded, or overlooked.

Instead, I am seen. I am known. I am loved.

Thank you, Jesus, for including me.

Amen.

Day 6

KILL KEYBOARDS WITH KINDNESS

I appeal to you, brothers and sisters, in the name of our Lord Jesus Christ, that all of you agree with one another in what you say and that there be no divisions among you, but that you be perfectly united in mind and thought.

1 CORINTHIANS 1:10

I was sitting at a table in our office when Jake showed me the article.

A church—yes, another *church*—in our city had written a negative article about me and our church, warning their congregation to stay away from ours.

There's a whole lot to unpack there that I do not have the space or time for, but the bottom line is that what was written was painful to read and detrimental to our shared Kingdom mission.

So much judgment. So many conclusions. So much taken out of context.

And the worst part? The person who wrote it—I have never met or known. A faceless person taking shots at me and my congregation online. I was understandably angry.

But after processing through my initial reaction, I worked up the courage to hold this man's words before the Lord. And I asked Jesus to help me forgive him. Over time, I have prayed often for that church and have asked God to bless them.

The Bible is a bit less technologically advanced than we are nowadays. So, unfortunately, it doesn't address this situation. However, there is a story in 1 Kings 19 that feels like a bit of an equivalent. Here's the scoop.

Elijah—a prophet of Yahweh—had recently embarrassed, belittled, and then slaughtered a group of prophets of Baal (a pagan god) on Mount Carmel. It was a seismic showing of God's power that is worth reading.[1]

But afterward, we read this: "So Jezebel sent a messenger to Elijah to say, 'May the gods deal with me, be it ever so severely, if by this time tomorrow I do not make your life like that of one of [the slaughtered prophets].'"[2]

The rhetoric here is harsh. But I wonder if, in our cultural moment, similar language has become commonplace. We see "keyboard warriors," as they're called, antagonizing others daily. Perhaps you've been on the receiving end of that.

Maybe you can recall the Instagram DM calling you names you hope never get repeated. Or the Twitter comments that crossed the line and looped in family members. Or even messages you received threatening violence.

A lot of damage has taken place, and a lot of hate has been spewed via keyboards and touch screens. The words "spoken" over us can linger for a long time. If you've been subject to hurtful online exchanges, I am so sorry.

The fact of the matter is that this is the world we live in. Unless we want to go completely off the grid (don't tempt me), then we must have at least some engagement with others online. And online engagement means opening up to strangers who can assume far too much.

Let's return to our story about Elijah. How did he respond to Jezebel's threat? "Elijah was afraid and ran for his life."[3] Often, that can be our response as well. Or we run the opposite way, toward our opponent.

We call this response fight or flight. And most of us choose one or the other. We block, ignore, and delete others' opinions or type out defensive replies when challenged. Black-and-white conclusions rule the inter web. The more salacious, the better.

But I believe there is a third way available to us. A way of forgiveness and—when possible—reconciliation. Where space is held for nuance and conversation. Where curiosity overcomes cynicism.

In order for this to take place, we must be willing to recognize others as made in the image of God. The apostle Paul writes, "Our struggle is not against flesh and blood, but against the rulers, against the authorities, against the powers of this dark world and against the spiritual forces of evil in the heavenly realms."[4]

What would it look like for you—today—to hold someone you regularly interact with online before the Lord and pray a prayer of blessing over them?

What if you asked God to change your heart and attitude toward them and for an overwhelming sense of compassion to reign in any future interactions?

Perhaps more boldly, what if you asked to meet face-to-face? To move from behind the keyboard to around the table? Because it is there that transformation occurs.

Prayer

God,

You are the creator of all things.

You say that a tongue is like a small rudder that steers the ship of our lives.[5]

You know all the words that have been spoken about me—whether hurtful or uplifting.

You know what is true of me.

You know what is not.

So, Jesus, help me to discern between the two.

As I navigate the online landscape, may my interactions—so much as I can control—be peaceful and kind.

And when I am ridiculed or slandered, remind me that I am not to repay insult with insult. On the contrary, I am to repay insult with blessing.[6]

In doing so, may I forgive those who use words to tear others down—both online and in person.

I pray that they would discover the same love that I have from you.

Thank you, Jesus.

Amen.

Day 7

BEGINNING THE PROCESS

The Lord is faithful, and he will strengthen you and protect you from the evil one.

2 THESSALONIANS 3:3

October 16, 2005, was the worst day of my life up to that point.

We had just returned home from Sunday morning service. Dad had given the sermon, and people had been saved. All seemed right in the world. Until it wasn't.

A few minutes later, a scream so loud that it echoed through our house sent me sprinting down the staircase. Turns out it was Mom. Thankfully, she was okay (physically), but her soul had been ripped out.

The next thing I knew, my dad was walking out the front door with a pile of clothes under one arm and some dry cleaning draped over the other.

"Daddy, where are you going?"

"Daddy's leaving."

"To go where?"

The car door slammed shut, and my dad drove off. He was leaving to live with his mistress. He was leaving behind the life he no longer wanted. He was leaving *me*.[1]

The divorce rate is still sky-high (41 percent), but people are getting married less than ever before. The average lifespan of a first marriage is roughly eight years.[2]

All that to say, the odds that your story resembles my story above (in some way) is possible. I know many spouses who have split up over the years. The anger and resentment that can fester is disorienting.

If you've experienced divorce or infidelity in your family or in your marriage, then perhaps you can resonate with my conclusion: I wasn't wanted.

An event like this can elicit all sorts of questions and thoughts.

Was I not good enough?

Could I have been a better spouse?

Am I the problem?

The more time we have to process, the more—intellectually—we understand the often-complicated nature of the situation. But in our heart, those questions linger.

All this can swell into a wave of grief that—if never dealt with—can have a profound effect on how we relate to others moving forward.

So, today, I want to wade into the deep waters of forgiving the parent or spouse who cheated, was unfaithful, or left.

Where do we even begin?

Well, first understand that unfortunately I don't have the space to engage all the nuances or complexities of your specific situation. For further insight, it may be helpful to read part 1 of *Three Strikes, You're Forgiven*.

What I would like to offer this day is how to *begin* the process of forgiveness.

As I sifted through this over the years in my own life, I realized that I had to begin with honesty. I had to name, to God, my counselor, and my dad, how I was feeling. Honestly? I was feeling hatred. I was feeling anger. And I named that.

So, right now, name how you're feeling toward the person who was unfaithful in your life. Let it out. Tell God. Tell your counselor. If able or appropriate, tell the person who has hurt you.

Then, grieve. Acknowledge that an injustice has taken place. Maybe you haven't given yourself space to acknowledge the damage that has been done in your family due to infidelity. Take time to process the loss in your life. Often infidelity can feel like death. The person is there one day and gone the next. It is a difficult reality to sort through.

Jesus longs for us to rebuild our broken relationships toward wholeness, restoration, and reconciliation. However, this takes time. And over time, trust must be earned back. If it's not, reconciliation is off the table. But forgiveness never is. Forgiveness is a constant invitation before you. You can choose today to forgive the person who walked out of your life.

That does not mean the relationship can or should be restored immediately, though. Forgiveness doesn't mean forgetfulness. It also doesn't mean bondage to bitterness.

True, authentic forgiveness leads with a heart posture that desires reconciliation and restoration. That doesn't mean that trust will ever be fully earned back. But it does love and live with a desire and hope that it can be.

Prayer

Jesus,

I know that you are always faithful.

Even when my spouse wasn't, you are faithful.

Even when I wasn't, you are faithful.

I am so (insert emotion you're feeling).

I don't understand why this has happened.

You know the hurt, betrayal, and loss of trust that I am experiencing.

But Jesus, I know that you are near.

So, help me to be honest about how I am feeling.

Help me to place my burden on you.

As I process my experience, help me to discover a future where forgiveness is possible.

Remind me that forgiveness is not so much for the person who hurt me—but for my sake.

Life does not look anything like I thought it would. And that feels so unfair.

But Jesus, I do not want to hold on to bitterness and resentment.

So help me to release the hurt and lean in to your faithfulness.

Instill in me peace to move forward in a way that honors you.

Amen.

Day 8

A TRUE FRIEND

Friends come and friends go, but a true friend sticks by you like family.

PROVERBS 18:24, MSG

I was angry. No, I was hurt. Actually, I was feeling let down.

All these emotions and more spilled out toward my friend, Matt, on a dark Friday morning in November.

The prior few months had been a whirlwind for both Matt and me. The environment was ripe for stress. We had some brief small talk in the mostly empty coffee shop before I decided I'd had enough of being two-faced.

"Matt, I have something I need to talk to you about. I need to share with you some resentment I've been holding on to for the last few months toward you and Kass."

Matt's face surprisingly didn't scream, "I can't wait for you to tell me this." (Sarcasm, folks. Smile. It'll help ease the tension.)

"I understand where you're coming from, but some of these expectations were plainly unrealistic for where Kass and I found ourselves in this present moment," Matt said.

I was fuming at this point. But you know what? Matt was right.

Forgiveness was the last thing that I wanted to ask Matt for at the time. But it was also the thing I most wanted.

In this case, when I apologized, Matt graciously offered me three of the most powerful words on earth: "I forgive you."

Immediately, all the tension within me ceased. Restoration started to do its work. Matt and I were ready to begin our relationship again. This is just one example of many that I can recall reminding me of how grateful I am for committed friendships.

As Scripture says, "Friends come and friends go, but a true friend sticks by you like family." There are certainly friendships that remain constant and stable throughout your life. If you have a friendship like that, count yourself lucky! The majority of friendships do not operate this way. Many change, grow, evolve, or die out over time.

There are certainly lifelong friends, but many friendships are "seasonal" due to proximity, interest, or experience. This is natural and healthy, but it can be difficult to grasp this concept and grieve or let go of the friendship when it is time. Instead, resentments can build and bitterness grow.

So, if you're willing—bring to mind a few friendships in your life.

How have these relationships changed and shifted over the years? What new friends have come, and what old friends have gone?

Have you been able to slow down and reflect on these shifting dynamics and acknowledge the changes? Have you forgiven the friends who have drifted away? Have you even acknowledged that they've drifted away?

It is okay to be sad about friendships that have been lost. But it's important to forgive those friends when the timeline of the relationship doesn't match up with the hopes and dreams you had for it.

Life goes on, and new friends will come . . . and go.

Press into these relational changes and cultivate gratitude for the friendships that stick. They are a treasure to protect.

Prayer

God,

Thank you for the many friends who have come and gone in my life.

I know that you've placed people in my life specifically for times such as this.

I know that there are friends who will become family and stick around for the long haul.

Jesus, I ask that you help me to forgive those who I thought would be like family but turned out to be seasonal friends.

Thank you for the gift of time that I was able to have with them.

I praise you—in advance—for those who will become lifers. Those who will stick with me through the ups and downs, highs and lows.

Thank you for the friends who already have.

What an immense gift and privilege it is to be in relationship with others.

Bless my friendships, Lord Jesus.

Amen.

Day 9

A FATHER WHO NEVER FAILS

A father to the fatherless . . .

PSALM 68:5

It was H-O-R-S to nothing. In a game of H-O-R-S-E, this is the precipice of victory. As a thirteen-year-old, I had never beaten my dad in anything basketball-related. And he routinely reminded me of it.

This was the best chance I'd ever had.

Over the next fifteen minutes, my dad talked trash and attempted to psychologically throw me off my game. It worked. We were tied H-O-R-S to H-O-R-S. And then he shot the ball from our front door to the other side of our driveway where the goal was.

Swish. Nothing but net.

Lacking the strength to hit such a shot, I thrust everything I had with one arm toward the hoop and watched my ball sail over the backboard. I immediately ran inside, fighting back frustrated tears. Was I being a sore loser? Perhaps. But it was a marked moment for me. Another reminder that I would never measure up to my dad.

I spent so much of my childhood trying to win his approval, to measure up, to best him. And at virtually every level, I failed.

My dad—for the most part—was gracious. But he certainly had moments of frustration, of annoyance, of "Why can't you just do this like I did?" In those moments, I felt small, insignificant, and worthless.

Maybe you have similar memories with your dad—if he was around at all (a wound in and of itself). Perhaps he shamed, berated, or embarrassed you. These moments, over time, begin to accrue, and before we know it, we find ourselves in counseling trying to break generational patterns.

Clearly this hurt is something we need to process. And—I would argue—it is something we need to forgive.

The wounds that are not healed, we often repeat. I am not a father yet, but I have found myself "parenting" my wife, friends, and other people's kids in similar ways to how my dad did. Interrupting, irritability, and a short temper plague many of my relationships.

As I've done the work to sift through this, I've recognized the need to release my dad—who himself was poorly parented—from some of the unrealistic expectations I had placed on him and from some of the real mistakes he made. Over time, I have had to continually remove my dad from the idol-pedestal of my life.

Though your dad is a reflection (at his best) of our heavenly Father, he is not our heavenly Father. We have a Father who never fails. Who delights in you. Who is never too busy for you. Who will never leave nor forsake you. Who loves you and pursues you with all that he is and has.

Bring your father wounds to the Father and let him heal you. He is a Father to the fatherless. In some ways, that is all of us.

Prayer

Abba Father,

Thank you for the gift of getting to call you by such a name.

Thank you for the compassion, kindness, and love that you possess.

Thank you for succeeding where earthly fathers failed.

Thank you for being present where earthly fathers were absent.

Thank you for being tender where earthly fathers were unloving.

Father, I ask that you would meet me in my relationship with my father.

Help me to recognize the good that I want to carry on. Help me to also recognize what I do not want to repeat. Empower me to break the cycle of what my father has passed down to me.

Jesus, where I could choose bitterness, help me to explore what forgiveness for my father would look like.

Remind me that in forgiving, I am not letting him off the hook.

Instead, I am transferring judgment over to you, and I am choosing grace and reconciliation.

I'm choosing intimacy with you where I could choose distance.

Father, I ask that you would right-size for me what fatherhood is.

Where gaps exist, allow me to fill them with you—a Father to the fatherless.

Amen.

Day 10

IN HIS HANDS

Can a mother forget the baby at her breast and have no compassion on the child she has borne? Though she may forget, I will not forget you!

ISAIAH 49:15

I've always been a momma's boy. The oldest of five, born to my mom at age twenty—how could I not be?

However, as I got older, I began to see some cracks in the armor of my mom's character. This shouldn't come as a shock or surprise. My mother—like everyone else—is human. But for the majority of my life, I did not see her that way.

Leaving for college, getting engaged, and getting married became major separators for my mom and me. These life transitions made me realize that some changes needed to take place in our relationship. As I worked to detangle unhealthy relational dynamics, division, instead, arose.

I remember driving up to Michigan, just my mom and me, and bringing up some concerns I had regarding the way she was treating me and, more importantly, the girl I would be marrying the following month. Instead of receiving my carefully calculated critique with grace and humility, she responded with defensiveness. I got the message: *You are young and don't know what you're talking about. You are so ungrateful.*

Now, to clarify, my mom said none of these things *explicitly*. But *implicitly*, this is what I heard. By the time we arrived at our destination, we both had tearstained faces and weren't on speaking terms. It was the lowest point of our relationship.

But in a way, her disapproval of my decisions at the time made me crave her approval even more.

Looking back, I have immense compassion for my mom for that season of life. There was so much transition and change happening, and we were trying to navigate it the best we knew how. My wedding came in the midst of some significant personal upheaval in her own life. Hurt that had nothing to do with me.

That being said, the way she responded still hurt me, and I had to work on releasing my need for her approval for years to come.

Author Andrew Comiskey "likens the mother wound to having a heart like a strainer, no matter how much love is poured in, there's no capacity to retain it."[1]

Perhaps you can resonate.

The hurt you've accrued in this relationship is real, but it does not have to be how you are defined. God says—through the prophet Isaiah—"See, I have engraved you on the palms of my hands; your walls are ever before me."[2]

When I was little, someone gifted me a drawing of this verse. It depicted two hands cupped together (representing God) with my name etched on it.

Over the years, I have returned to that drawing as a reminder that God is both mother and father to perfection. He holds me, sees me, and loves me with all that he has.

Moses likens God to a mother eagle who stirs up its nest and hovers over its young.[3] Jesus says virtually the same thing.[4] Because both man and woman are made in God's image, both the father and mother role—in some way—image God.

Where your mom failed to give you the nurture, care, or attention that you needed, God never does. This truth has freed me to forgive my mom for the ways that she has fallen short. Because she is not perfect. God is. And he has me (and you) in the palm of his hands.

Prayer

Jehovah Rapha,

You are the God who heals.

And where my mother has fallen short, you, God, can heal.

Thank you for placing me in the palm of your hands.

Thank you for never giving up on me.

I ask that you would meet me in my relationship with my mother.

Help me to see the ways that my mom cared for me. Help me also to forgive her for not living into her call in all the ways she should have.

Give me grace and compassion to recognize the obstacles my mom had to overcome throughout her life.

I ask that you help me to break any destructive cycles that have been handed down from generation to generation in my family.

I long to chart a new course, to live a different way.

Let me begin with forgiveness, today.

Amen.

Day 11

FORGIVING AND LETTING GO

If it is possible, as far as it depends on you, live at peace with everyone.

ROMANS 12:18

Often on the journey of forgiveness, we can struggle to discern what is ours to hold and what is ours to let go.

For instance, perhaps you've walked through your spouse's infidelity that resulted in divorce, and now, you feel guilty that your children have to live in two different places. This is certainly something to grieve, but is it something *you* should feel guilty about? You were not the spouse who was unfaithful. Your choices did not create these consequences, unfortunate as they are.

This is one of the aspects that make working through forgiveness so complex. Do you forgive your unfaithful spouse and stay in relationship? Perhaps, if repentance is present along with a desire to turn around and to live in a different way. But what if it isn't? What if your spouse decides to lean further into the lifestyle that destroyed your marriage? Does forgiveness look like staying in relationship with them in that case? I don't think so. In this scenario, forgiveness may look like releasing them to the life they chose.[1]

Scripture has much to say about facing the consequences of our actions. For instance, in one of his letters Paul instructs the Corinthian church on how to respond regarding an instance where a man is sleeping with his father's wife. Paul tells them that if this man is unrepentant and continues to live sinfully, they should "hand this man over to Satan for the destruction of the flesh, so that his spirit may be saved on the day of the Lord."[2]

On the surface, this seems incredibly harsh. But there's actually inherent beauty here. Notice how Paul finishes his refrain: "So that his spirit may be saved." Paul's not looking to humiliate the man; he's looking to redeem him, but redemption can only occur when consequences are experienced. This is why we call it a "comeback." There's a return, usually from rock bottom. This can be the most gracious, loving aspect of our forgiveness journey. If we do not let go of our sin, then we enslave ourselves to the very thing causing us harm.

The consequences of someone else's wrong choices affecting you is the tragic result of living in a fallen world. One day, sin will be eradicated. In the meantime, we are to work toward peace.

I love how the apostle Paul frames it. He says, "If it is possible, as far as it depends on you, live at peace with everyone."

His language is incredibly pastoral. First, *if it is possible*.

If repentance is present, restoration is possible. But it takes time, and it's a two-way street. Forgiveness is a solo sport.[3] You alone can choose to forgive the person who hurt you. Reconciliation is a bit more nuanced.

Next, *as far as it depends on you*. Reconciliation takes two to tango. The person you're attempting to reconcile with may want no part of it. If that's the case, then restoration is virtually impossible. But this is not your fault. So, release your feelings of guilt.

And finally, *live at peace with everyone*.

Notice Paul does not tell us to live intimately with everyone, in proximity to everyone, fearfully with everyone, boundaryless with everyone, excusing everyone. No! He says to live at peace—so much as it depends on you.

My friend, who do you need to forgive today? Write the letter. Send the text. Make the call. So much as it depends on you, work toward peace. But so much as it does not depend on you, release the situation to King Jesus, trusting that he works all things for good.

Prayer

Abba Father,

I know that you see me in the current complexity of life.

Would you give me discernment to sort out what is mine to carry and what is mine to let go?

I am in need of your wisdom.

My present circumstances are the result of someone else's choices.

This grieves, angers, and frustrates me.

Yet, I have a choice. I can choose bitterness or forgiveness.

Help me to choose the latter today, Jesus.

So much as it depends on me, help me to work toward peace.

Thank you for your grace and understanding, for acknowledging that in some circumstances—perhaps my circumstance—it is not possible to restore the relationship.

You know that reconciliation takes two who are willing to pursue wholeness.

The person I am working to forgive is not there.

So, once I am ready to forgive, if it is still not possible to pursue peace, help me to release them, entrusting their future to you, the God who sees all.

Amen.

Day 12

SET FREE

You are no longer a slave, but God's child; and since you are his child, God has made you also an heir.

GALATIANS 4:7

In the summer of 2016, my parents received a text from an adoption agency worker attending their church. My parents had always had open conversations with us about adopting one day. However, at this point in time, my folks were less than a year into a church plant here in Indianapolis and were not in a position to adopt a child. Nonetheless, this particular text message would change everything . . .

After the initial text, an additional email was sent to my parents: a profile of two young kids, a boy (age nine) and a girl (age seven). They were the oldest of five kids from Indianapolis who were being put up for adoption by their struggling single mother. To this day, I so admire the courage of this mom to offer her children a better life than she could provide. Up until this point, their life had been difficult. Hardship was baked into these two tiny humans.

My parents opened that email on a Thursday, and we met the birth mom and children at Chuck E. Cheese the following Monday. That's right. Four days later. My parents ended up receiving emergency custody of my now-siblings on June 22, 2016. The initial process was complete in under three weeks. Warp speed for any adoption.

Because the process was so fast, no one in our family was ready for the lives we were inheriting. There was very little background information given by the adoption agency because they didn't have it. We were simply elated to be adding two beautiful children to our family. However, with time, they began to open up to us about their troubled early childhood years.

Their lives were so transient, I wasn't sure how they could keep all the different apartments, shelters, and cars they had slept in straight. With each meal, they would share another story that would make all our stomachs churn and cause us to lose our appetites. My father would ask compassionate, curious questions, but with each answer, I could see my parents getting more and more worked up. These kids were their kids now, and they felt a duty to protect them.

It has been a painful, difficult journey of healing for both of them. But they're doing the work. And it has been beautiful and heartwarming to see the amount of time, attention, love, and devotion my parents have shown them in helping them to forgive the hurt of their past and to move forward with the new future that lies before them.

Adoption is unique because it is chosen. This matters because God adopted us. He *chose* us. Those of us who were once in bondage have been set free.

Where are you needing freedom today? Are you willing to enter into the messy and arduous, but beautiful and necessary, process of forgiving others and allowing Christ to form you?

Perhaps you have become enslaved to bitterness, over time finding yourself more irritable and angry with every person you encounter. You long for peace and kindness to be restored in your soul.

Maybe you've thrown yourself into cynicism, and the summation of your life and relationships is marked by a "glass-half-empty" mentality. Today, you need Jesus to renew you with fresh perspective, hope, and optimism for your future.

Perhaps you've held on to resentment and become consumed by competition, constantly comparing your life to others' and never feeling satisfied or content. Today, you need Jesus to help you forgive others for the ways you've felt let down, abandoned, or hurt.

Could there be a better way? A way of life that brings the fulfillment, security, love, forgiveness, and freedom you've been longing for?

There is! It's through Jesus. It's by renouncing all other idols in your life and pledging your allegiance to him. It's through repentance—turning around and going a different way, placing your faith and trust in Jesus. Understand that there is never enough you can do to earn his love. It's already been freely given. You have been chosen—adopted—by a Father who sees you.

Prayer

Father God,

I praise you, as I am reminded that you chose me.

At my worst.

At my lowest.

In my pride, rebellion, and sin.

You came down to earth, inserted yourself into our story, and saved us.

God, that would have been enough. But rather than simply saving us, you restored right relationship with us.

You chose me. I am your child.

Thank you for extending forgiveness.

Thank you for your sacrifice.

Thank you for setting me free.

Thank you for always welcoming the repentant prodigal home.

Here I come.

Amen.

PART II

Asking for Forgiveness

Day 13

SPEAK LIFE

Keep your tongue from evil and your lips from telling lies.

PSALM 34:13

I didn't grow up in a home where cuss words were thrown around. In fact, I rarely—if ever—heard my parents use unwholesome language in front of my brothers and me.

But as I entered the foray of public school, I was introduced to a whole new vocabulary.

One day, I couldn't wait to share a new word I had learned with a few of my friends. We had indoor recess, and our teacher gave us some extra liberty to roam the halls. After a quick bathroom break, I came around the corner and—with all the confidence in the world—yelled, "What the hell are you guys talking about?"

"Mr. Davis?"

Instead of my friends who I'd left a few minutes ago, there stood my teacher.

"What did you just say?"

"Uh, nothing."

"Excuse me?"

"Heck! I said heck!"

"Look me in the eyes and tell me what you said."

"I said heck!"

It is I. A bold-faced liar. I compounded an already sinful situation by lying about the fact that I had cursed.

I look back on that story now and laugh, but unfortunately it wasn't the last time that I told an outright lie. And as I got older, some of those lies had far bigger consequences than a time-out at recess. Perhaps you know all too well how lies can spiral out of control.

One instance of compounded deception in Scripture is the story of two brothers: Jacob and Esau. In Genesis 27, Jacob takes advantage of his father's poor sight and lies to him. He wears his brother Esau's clothes and puts goatskin on his hands and neck to mimic the hair he does not have. As he goes to his father, the Scriptures say, "*Jacob* said to his father, 'I am Esau your firstborn. I have done as you told me. Please sit up and eat some of my game, so that you may give me your blessing.'"[1]

And that's exactly what happens. Jacob, the second born, steals the blessing of Esau—the firstborn—via a lie.

That lie ends up costing both brothers a great deal of pain in the years to come. An initial lie, which spirals into more lies, causes immense relational harm.[2]

Since the beginning of time, we have been deceived and participated in deceiving one another and ourselves.

It is estimated that the average person tells one to two lies per day.[3] That comes out to over seven hundred lies per year.

All that to say, it's certain that we have lied and been lied about. The ancient proverb states, "The mouth of the righteous is a fountain of life."[4] And yet, we have probably spoken more death than we'd care to admit.

So, perhaps today, *we* need to ask for forgiveness. Forgiveness for the things we've said that we shouldn't have. Forgiveness for things spoken that were untrue. Forgiveness for the ways we've exaggerated or misspoken or used coarse language.

To pursue reconciliation is to pursue wholeness. We can't become whole, holy, and healthy people without words to match.

Prayer

Holy Spirit,

I want to be a person who speaks life.

In a world filled with lies, I want to be a person of truth.

I am sorry for the ways I've used my tongue for ill rather than for good.

There have been moments when I've been tempted to exaggerate, misinform, or mislead to gain attention, acceptance, or approval.

Forgive me for the misplaced desires of my heart.

Jesus, help me to catch myself when I am on the verge of saying something that doesn't reflect your grace, kindness, and love.

Help me to use my speech for good.

Amen.

Day 14

CONFESSION

Confess your sins to each other and pray for each other so that you may be healed. The prayer of a righteous person is powerful and effective.

JAMES 5:16

In pastoral meetings with individuals struggling with forgiveness, I often tell them that the key to asking for forgiveness is actually a practice known as confession. That may seem counterintuitive, but hear me out.

When we look at the life of Jesus and the Scriptures as a whole, we see that confession is a central theme. For instance, take the book of Psalms—specifically, Psalms 6, 32, 38, 51, 102, 130, and 143. These are known as the penitential psalms or the psalms of *confession*.

All throughout Jesus' ministry, he encountered people who desired healing. In an effort to receive healing, they *confessed* their brokenness. Listen to the language used in Matthew 15: "Lord, son of David, have mercy on me."[1]

Or in Luke 17: "Jesus, Master, have pity on us!"[2]

Or in Matthew 20: "Lord, Son of David, have mercy on us!"[3]

We could keep going, but the commonality is that in each of these instances, people came before Jesus broken and humble, asking Jesus to do what only he can do—overcome their deficiencies and make them whole.

What if we were to see our spiritual deficiencies and approach Jesus with the same mindset as these people did with their physical limitations?

What if this sort of posture—a broken and contrite heart, as the psalmist calls it in Psalm 51—is the only posture where true forgiveness can take root?[4]

The apostle John writes, "If we confess our sins, He is faithful and just to forgive us our sins and to cleanse us from all unrighteousness."[5]

So, we confess our sins to God, and in return, God forgives us and mercifully cleanses us to return into right relationship with him. This is a beautiful paradigm.

Now, I want to note a distinction here. John writes that if we confess our sins (presumably to God), he is faithful to forgive us. But James says that when we confess our sins to one another, we are healed.

I believe this is intentional. See, in our individualized way of life, many of us are walking around forgiven but wounded. Holy but hurting. Because we've normalized confessing to God but have avoided confessing to one another at all costs. And in avoiding the practice, we've missed out on opportunities to discover the real power of forgiveness.

Confession can be a conduit to break free of the shame that sin holds over us.

Confession—at its best—is an acknowledgment of sin before God and our brothers and sisters in Christ, a humble request for forgiveness, and a commitment to live differently henceforth, while accepting the consequences our actions have incurred.

So, what if, in order to grow in your capacity to forgive, you first need to grow in your capacity to confess?

There is nothing that heals quite like confessing sin to someone and hearing them say, "Micah, you are forgiven."

Give it a try. No matter their response, when you confess, you are forgiven by God. What a wonderful truth!

Prayer

El Shaddai,

You are the Lord God Almighty.

You somehow hold all things together.

There is nothing you don't see or hear.

So, why do I pretend like I can hide from you?

Instead, I want to turn toward you and go a different way from how I've been living.

I want to live full of freedom and peace.

I want to come out of the dark and step into the light.

I know that confession helps me to do so.

Father, grant me the courage to specifically name my sin to someone other than you.

I know that when I confess to you, I am forgiven, but when I confess to others, I experience healing.

As relational beings, this is how you have formed and fashioned us, and it is oh, so beautiful.

May I discover that beauty for myself, this day.

Amen.

Day 15

ASK

Have mercy on me, O God, according to your unfailing love;
according to your great compassion blot out my transgressions.
Wash away all my iniquity and cleanse me from my sin.

PSALM 51:1-2

Forgiveness is a decision. But forgiveness is also a process. Where do we begin when asking for forgiveness?

Well, first we must begin with remorse. In order to authentically receive forgiveness, we must be genuinely sorry for what we have done or who we have hurt.

We must feel the magnitude and weight of our sin. This is a good thing. God does not bring us face-to-face with our sin to shame or condemn us. As the apostle Paul writes, "There is now no condemnation for those who are in Christ Jesus, because through Christ Jesus the law of the Spirit who gives life has set you free from the law of sin and death."[1] Instead, when we face our sin, we see God's holiness—and how much we are forgiven. We long to be made right through relationship with him.

After expressing remorse, we must commit to recourse. We are enabled to choose a new way of life. In the Scriptures, this is referred to as repentance.

In Greek, to repent is the word *metanoeō*, and it means to turn around or to go another direction.[2] Receiving forgiveness from someone we've hurt, wounded, or upset should motivate us to change. If not, we are not loving our neighbor as ourselves. Instead, the cycle of hurt will only be prolonged.

To repent—to turn around—is actionable. Recourse means taking responsibility for the ways we've fallen short and intentionally choosing to live differently.

If repentance is present, then recommitment is necessary.

In our journey of forgiveness, there will come a time when temptation to return to our old ways surfaces. It's in those moments that we must regularly recommit to the new way of life that we have chosen. Daily, we surrender our pride, pick up our cross, and follow Jesus.

Humility is at the heart of forgiveness. We forgive because we have been forgiven. When we receive undeserved forgiveness from others, it is only possible because God gave each of us undeserved forgiveness himself.

Embracing forgiveness can't be done alone, however. Community is central.

The boat you're rowing isn't powerful enough to go upstream in the river that is our world. We have to be willing to get into the boat with others and—by the power of the Holy Spirit—row together for the sake of authentic witness of the gospel—the Good News of Jesus Christ—to the world.

Lastly, in asking for and receiving forgiveness, we must restore trust and credibility. The only currency we have in this part of the process is time.

Forgiveness can be instant. Trust and healing happen gradually.

Restoration takes place one piece—one day—at a time. Look for daily invitations to rebuild trust with the person you have hurt. Days, weeks, and months after they've forgiven you, they still need and deserve to be shown that you care for and love them. Our actions must match our words.

If this sounds difficult, it is. But it's necessary. And it's good, true, and beautiful.

So, if you find yourself in the wrong today, don't wait. Ask God to reveal the ways you've fallen short, and express remorse. Then choose to go a different way. Recommit to this new way of life. And as you live into the "new creation" that you are, ask God to restore what has been broken and make it whole.

Prayer

Lord Jesus,

"What I want to do I do not do, but what I hate I do."[3]

I confess that I have fallen short.

Have mercy on me.

Reveal to me the ways that I am being held back from who you've called me to be.

And as you do, would you allow your kindness to lead me to repentance?

I want to live a different way.

So, Jesus, help me to choose that way, today. And tomorrow. And the next day.

All the days of my life, lead me in the way everlasting.

When I am tempted to return to my old ways, grant me the strength to recommit to living freely and lightly.

Help me to be transformed in my relationships.

To be quick to listen and slow to speak.

I confess that I have sinned against you and my neighbor.

Thank you for already forgiving me.

May my heart posture be one of remorse, recourse, recommitment, and restoration.

Amen.

Day 16

COME INTO THE LIGHT

If we claim to be without sin, we deceive ourselves and the truth is not in us. If we confess our sins, he is faithful and just and will forgive us our sins and purify us from all unrighteousness. If we claim we have not sinned, we make him out to be a liar and his word is not in us.

1 JOHN 1:8-10

When my sister was little, she had a knack for lying. But not just lying. She could convince you by the end of the conversation that whatever she was being accused of, you'd made up.

One time, my dad watched her grab a pen from someone's desk. When he called her out on it, she acted like he was seeing things. My dad asked, "Are you telling me that I didn't just watch you take a pen from that desk?"

"Yes."

When my dad made her empty her pockets, of course the pen was there. It's a humorous memory now, but don't we often do the same thing with God? Rather than confess when we mess up, we try to hide our actions from him—even though he already knows.

The apostle John writes, "If we claim to be without sin, we deceive ourselves and the truth is not in us."

There will come a day when you mess up, fall short, sin. It may be later today, tomorrow, or next week that you miss the mark. When you do, what comes next?

The temptation will be to hide, as Adam and Eve did in the garden. When confronted, our instinct is to deceive or blame.

But what stays in the dark stays dark. Jesus puts it this way: "If then the light within you is darkness, how great is that darkness!"[1]

In other words, when we attempt to convince ourselves or others that our sin is not sin, we're merely deceiving ourselves, compounding the hold that sin has on us.

Perhaps today you've messed up. You've fallen short. You've given in.

This is not the end of the story. Before you lies a choice, to come clean or to hide.

Hiding will only grow the darkness. Coming clean brings something maybe more difficult but certainly less painful in the long run: Freedom. Purity. Forgiveness.

John continues, "If we confess our sins, he is faithful and just and will forgive us our sins and purify us from all unrighteousness."

Notice the causal relationship.

If we confess, he forgives.

My friend, God already knows what you've done. The psalmist of Psalm 147 writes that God's understanding is infinite.[2] There's nowhere to hide. And that is a beautiful reality. Because waiting for us on the other side is not punishment—Jesus took that on for us on the cross—but purification. Correction may be needed, but forgiveness is also extended. It is God's kindness that leads us to repentance.

So, come into the light. As the apostle John writes, "Whoever lives by the truth comes into the light, so that it may be seen plainly that what they have done has been done in the sight of God."[3] If you've messed up, acknowledge it. Confess it. Let God be faithful and just to show you mercy. To offer forgiveness.

Prayer

Merciful God,

You know that I long to follow you and to practice your way.

But the thoughts I've had, the words I've said, the actions I've taken, sometimes do not align with the person you desire for me to become.

So, Jesus, I'm sorry when I miss the mark.

But here in your presence, my true self is being reflected back to me.

In the mirror I see who I want to be, who I can be, should I continue to abide in you.

Jesus, root out the darkness within, forgive me, and help me to live continually in the light.

Weeping may stay for the night, but joy comes with the morning.[4]

Amen.

Day 17

A NEW MARRIAGE

Because of this oath, Jesus has become the guarantor of a better covenant.

HEBREWS 7:22

In my opinion, the hardest and best part of marriage is the amount of forgiveness you will give and receive. There is something about a healthy, covenantal relationship that echoes the very gospel we preach: a wayward people pursued by a lovestruck God. People who hurt God over and over again and yet are forgiven over and over again.

I have seen a similar pattern play out in my own marriage (and covenant friendships, too; this is for all of us).

While Rylei is human and makes mistakes, too, I am easily the one who is apologizing more. That's not because I'm better at asking; it's because I say more stupid things.

And yet, over the course of our marriage, each hurt has been absolved by forgiveness. As a result, our love is stronger than ever.

Instead of allowing these moments to fuel resentment toward one another, we've prioritized healing.

I set out at the beginning of each day with the intention of honoring my wife. But inevitably, at some point, I act in a way that is misaligned with the love, joy, peace, patience, kindness, goodness, faithfulness, gentleness, and self-control that I am supposed to exhibit. At every turn, though, when Rylei or I could walk away, we've leaned in. This response—to pursue reconciliation rather than division—has strengthened and fortified our love and devotion toward one another.

I believe the same can be true of our relationship with God. He has covenanted himself to us through Jesus.[1] His love for us is endless.[2] He is faithful to forgive and purify us when we confess our sins.[3]

Perhaps you have made many mistakes in your life. I certainly have. Maybe relationships have crumbled around you. Maybe you are the reason for a lot of hurt and pain.

If this is the case, know that you are not alone. There is someone who is ready and willing to forgive you.

Who will never leave or forsake you.[4]

Who loves you today, tomorrow, and every day into the future.

The hardest and best part of marriage is the amount of forgiveness you will give and receive. A day is coming when a new marriage between heaven and earth will take place and forgiveness—rather than failure—will be final. Reconciliation will be the eternal, everlasting ending to the Story that is being written.

This is good news, indeed.

Prayer

Holy Spirit,

I thank you that you are just and faithful to intercede for me.

There are many hurts that I am responsible for.

Yet, I am forgiven over and over again.

I look forward, with great expectation, to the wedding that is to come.

A marriage that will look like the perfect version of my most intimate relationship here on earth.

The person I am closest to has likely had to forgive me the most.

But in the age to come, we will experience eternal reconciliation.

A wedding feast will begin.

All that is broken will be restored.

Amen.

Day 18

FALLING FORWARD

All have sinned and fall short of the glory of God, and all are justified freely by his grace through the redemption that came by Christ Jesus.

ROMANS 3:23-24

When I was in third grade, I played baseball for the first and last time. It was the first year of what's referred to as "live pitching," where the players themselves pitch. I played for the Noblesville Yankees. I was stoked to get to don such a legendary logo. Every time I laced up my cleats, I'd imagine I was Derek Jeter on deck at Yankee Stadium.

Unfortunately, the season was a disaster. I was the only kid on the team who never got a chance to "live pitch." My coach kindly but clearly communicated that my arm wasn't strong enough. I was a year younger than all of my peers and developmentally wasn't close to being skilled enough to hang with the older kids. I was relegated to right field (the area of a baseball field where one is least likely to be involved in the action).

I also spent the entire season swinging and missing.

That's right. The entire season, I never got a hit. Well, that's not technically true. The last game of the season, I contributed to a run via a "sacrifice bunt" where (honestly accidentally) my bat made brief contact with the ball, allowing a teammate to score. Later in that game, I also was "walked" (this happens when the pitcher throws four pitches outside of the strike zone) and eventually found myself "stealing" home on an errant throw. It was exhilarating but unfulfilling.

Why?

Because the rest of the season? Bat after bat . . . it was the same story over and over again.

I would swing and miss. Swing and miss. Swing and miss.

And every time, the teenage, minimum-wage umpire would cruelly caw, "Three strikes, you'reeeeee out!"

Perhaps you've come to a point in your journey of forgiveness where you feel like you can never get it right. Every time you're up to bat, you swing and miss. Maybe you're reading this, holding your breath at the idea that you—*you* of *all* people—could ever be forgiven for what you've done. Maybe you're filled with shame, regret, or embarrassment for the failures of your past. Maybe you feel like your life has consisted of strikeout after strikeout.

To those of you who feel like you could never be forgiven, hear King David's words in Psalm 103:

> He has not dealt with us according to our sins, nor punished us according to our iniquities. For as the heavens are high above the earth, so great is His mercy

> toward those who fear Him; as far as the east is from the west, so far has He removed our transgressions from us. As a father pities his children, so the LORD pities those who fear Him.
>
> **PSALM 103:10-13, NKJV**

Friend, whatever it is that you've done, whatever it is that you fell short in, whatever it is that you messed up, God *forgives* you. As high as the heavens are above the earth, as far as the east is from the west, so great is his mercy . . . to you and to me. You are forgiven—in Christ Jesus—saved by the blood of the cross.

Paul writes to the Romans, "All have sinned and fall short of the glory of God, and all are justified freely by his grace through the redemption that came by Christ Jesus."[1]

The invitation of Jesus—the way of forgiveness—is a high, high bar. But there is grace, grace, grace. Not to abdicate responsibility, but to try and fail. We must normalize messing up. Getting it wrong. Falling short. Are we putting in the effort? Are we showing up? Are we falling *forward*?

There is respite for your soul available. No matter what you've done or what's been done to you, there exists a better way. It is not a way devoid of suffering or pain. And it is not an easy three-step process. Practicality in the arena of forgiveness is scarce. It is a journey full of starts and stops. Two steps forward and three steps back. It is a long, narrow way. But it is a way of breakthrough, of healing, and of triumph.

It's the way of Jesus. To you and to me, he offers an invitation.

> Are you tired? Worn out? Burned out on religion? Come to me. Get away with me and you'll recover your life. I'll show you how to take a real rest. Walk with me and work with me—watch how I do it. Learn the unforced rhythms of grace. I won't lay anything heavy or ill-fitting on you. Keep company with me and you'll learn to live freely and lightly.
>
> **MATTHEW 11:28-30, MSG**

When the going gets tough . . .

When the odds are stacked against you . . .

When you've been let down repeatedly . . .

When you've failed over and over again . . . the Umpire of life's voice screams out, "Three strikes, you'reeeeee . . . *forgiven*."

There is grace to try again.

Prayer

Merciful Father,

I am so thankful for your grace.

Today, tomorrow, and on into forever, you gently say, "Try again."

There are starts and stops.

Crashes and falls.

. . . but eventually, breakthrough.

Thank you, Jesus, for your blood.

The reason we can experience breakthrough in the first place.

And that is my prayer this day.

May I not just know—theoretically—about your unending grace, but may I experience—tangibly—your unending grace today.

Lord, Jesus Christ, have mercy on me, a sinner.

Jesus, envelop me in your mercy.

And may that mercy spur me on to try again, and again, and again, as I seek to become the person of love, joy, and peace you intended.

Amen.

Day 19

A VISION FOR COUPLES

Wives, submit yourselves to your own husbands as you do to the Lord. . . . Husbands, love your wives, just as Christ loved the church and gave himself up for her.

EPHESIANS 5:22, 25

There's perhaps no relationship on earth that causes more pain and more joy than a marital relationship. The covenanting of two individuals becoming one is both a sacred and weighty proposition.

The Bible itself underscores the unique commitment of marriage in several places. Ephesians 5 is one of my favorite Scripture passages to turn to where this is parsed out.

Many get hung up on the idea of submission that Paul expounds upon and miss the challenge to husbands to give themselves up for their wives. It's also easy to overlook that this passage is couched by two verses that serve as the frame for the picture that is marriage. Verse 21 says, "Submit to one another out of reverence for Christ."[1] And verse 33: "Each one of you also must love his wife as he loves himself, and the wife must respect her husband."[2]

My point is this: The glue that holds marriage together is *mutuality*.

This is not a contract between coach and player, person 1A and 1B, the boss and the subject. Such visions of marriage are—quite honestly—antithetical to the Scriptures.

The vision of marriage that Scripture paints, not just in Ephesians 5, but as it was intended in Genesis 2, is one of equality *and* particularity. We are equal, yes, but we are also distinct in the gifts, talents, abilities, personalities, and offerings we have and can give one another. Reframing marriage in this light, I believe, reveals the heavenly beauty the covenant is intended to reflect.

Still, such a vision of marriage does not protect anyone from hurt. There will be days when your spouse says or does something that cuts deeply. There will be days when the feelings of love, attraction, and desire wane. And yes, there will be days when you question whether putting in the effort is worth it.

As Rylei and I have counseled couples over the years, we've determined that it is in these moments one must choose forgiveness. These small cuts, over time, if not dealt with, can quickly build up resentment and bitterness toward your spouse. Thankfully, the opposite is also true. When you choose forgiveness, greater intimacy with your spouse can be experienced and a picture of marriage, as it was intended to be, is revealed.

This is not to say that every offense deserves a conversation. But every offense does deserve observation. Become aware of the relational dynamics of your marriage, and ask yourself if you are actively walking in the way of forgiveness.

Couples—because of the intimate nature of their relationship—can quickly become wounded healers. We are given opportunities to serve as a prophetic witness to the world around us of what a reconciled relationship looks like. The more we are able to practice daily forgiveness, the better we protect our marriage from larger hurts down the road.

There's a reason Paul says, "Do not let the sun go down while you are still angry."[3] It isn't to say that we can't ever feel angry or hurt. It means that we should—so much as it depends on us—work toward forgiveness.

Couples, we have an opportunity to exemplify unconditional love that is built on a foundation of forgiveness and scaled—brick by brick—by consistent reconciliation. As we move toward one another, our love grows and matures, and the world learns the true power of Christlike love.

Prayer

Dear Jesus,

Today I place my spouse before you.

You know them intimately, inside and out, better than I ever could.

Thank you for the ways you have uniquely wired my spouse.

Help me to discern how best to love them.

I confess that sometimes I have fallen short in fulfilling my vows, allowing resentment or hurt to have the last word.

There have been days I have withheld love in my actions and words.

Forgive me, Father. And help me, this day, to turn around and to live differently.

Holy Spirit, I also sense you bringing to mind the ways that I have been hurt.

Forgive my spouse, and help me to forgive them.

Remind me that forgiveness bridges distance in our relationship.

When I am tempted to withdraw, help me to lean in.

And as I go first in consciously choosing this way of reconciliation, help me to love my spouse as you love them.

Amen.

Day 20

NOT TOO LATE

Fathers, do not exasperate your children; instead, bring them up in the training and instruction of the Lord.

EPHESIANS 6:4

"Parents, you will be the primary reason your kid needs counseling growing up." Some version of this statement is a common refrain that I've heard in multiple church circles.

The fact of the matter is that parents find themselves in a close and proximate relationship with their children that lasts (usually) for eighteen years. One of the primary differences between a parental relationship and other types of relationships is the overt power dynamics that exist. Parents are the primary caregivers of their child. From birth, they are responsible for keeping their child *alive*. While children live under their parents' roof, formation and maturation take place. And so, too, does wounding. This isn't avoidable. Even the best parents unintentionally cause hurt in their children's lives.

If you are a parent, take a moment to consider what you would like to rectify in your parenting journey.

Perhaps you can think of instances you lost your temper. Maybe you are grieving seasons of distance or silence. Or perhaps years of absence define your relationship.

Whatever it may be, allow the Spirit to draw you into those moments. Spend some time acknowledging the ways you fell short and how you would like to improve your relationship with your children in the future. Consider writing them down now.

Sitting in that tension, think of Joseph and how his own family conspired to kill him and ended up selling him into slavery.[1] I have a hunch that you haven't done anything that egregious to hurt any of your family members.

Years later, God brought Joseph into power, and eventually, he came face-to-face with his brothers again. Joseph's response is stunning. He said, "Do not be distressed and do not be angry with yourselves for selling me here, because it was to save lives that God sent me ahead of you."[2]

Somehow, Joseph was able to see the bigger story being written, despite the wounding and family betrayal. Joseph's brothers did not stop God from using Joseph in the capacity he wanted to. In fact, some would argue that God used Joseph's family to position Joseph where he was supposed to be all along![3]

Dear parent, know that your child is in God's hands. Your shortcomings can't stop God from using your son or daughter the way that he intends to. Perhaps you have contributed to the hurt your child is feeling. If you've been parenting for any longer than one minute, this is almost surely the case. If so, take the memories you've jotted down, bring them before your child, and apologize.

Humbly approaching your children in a spirit of repentance will speak volumes. That will do as much to shape them as your mistakes—if not more.

I can recall two different "dads" I had growing up. One was my dad before his extramarital affair, and the other was my dad after. My dad after was broken and contrite. He was quick to apologize and genuinely remorseful when he fell short. Those moments of apology are what stick out in my mind, not so much the moments of disappointment.

Parents, it's not too late to apologize. If you are estranged or have not talked for some time, you can still pick up the phone, make the call, send the text. Initiate a conversation. Those dynamics I referenced earlier are in play, even if your child is grown and nothing egregious has happened. Your son or daughter being able to witness you model Christlike humility will mark them.

As you relax into God's presence today, hear the Word of the Lord, which says, "Be kind and compassionate to one another, forgiving each other, just as in Christ God forgave you."[4]

Maybe you do find yourself in a situation where reconciliation seems genuinely impossible right now. If that is the case, understand that forgiveness is still available. Even if your child is unwilling to offer it, know that you—in Christ—are forgiven. Today is an invitation to turn around, to go another way, and to be—as the apostle Paul says—a new creation.[5]

Trust that you did not get in the way of God's plan for your child's life. No, my friend, you *are* God's plan for your child's life.[6] No one can ever replace you as a mom or dad. You may have stumbled in the past, but God can redeem it. You may be struggling in the present, but God can restore it. You may be fearful of the future, but God has secured it. Forgiveness is available to you today. Live in that freedom.

Prayer

Abba Father,

Thank you for being the perfect parent.

Thank you for the ways that you have guided, guarded, and led my child.

You know that I have made mistakes in my parenting journey.

I am sorry for the ways I have rejected or forgotten who you've called me to be.

I long to exercise well the power and authority you've entrusted to me.

Help me to navigate this road with wisdom, prudence, patience, and discernment.

When I mess up, give me the humility to be quick to apologize and to ask for forgiveness.

May my repentant spirit be a model that my children follow.

And even if they do not, remind me that I am not a hindrance but an imperfect vehicle to my child's flourishing.

Give me your eyes to see my son or daughter the way you see them.

I entrust their life to you.

Amen.

Day 21

REWRITING THE SCRIPT

When they had finished eating, Jesus said to Simon Peter, "Simon son of John, do you love me more than these?" "Yes, Lord," he said, "you know that I love you." Jesus said, "Feed my lambs."

JOHN 21:15

Forgiveness is always possible. It's not always fair, but it's *always* possible.

A few days after Jesus' death, burial, and resurrection, the Lord appears to Peter. This is the first recorded conversation we have between them since Peter's tragic failure in Mark 14, and here's how it goes:

> "Simon son of John, do you love me more than these?"
>
> "Yes, Lord," he said, "you know that I love you."
>
> Jesus said, "Feed my lambs."
>
> Again Jesus said, "Simon son of John, do you love me?"
>
> He answered, "Yes, Lord, you know that I love you."
>
> Jesus said, "Take care of my sheep."
>
> The third time he said to him, "Simon son of John, do you love me?"

> Peter was hurt because Jesus asked him the third time, "Do you love me?" He said, "Lord, you know all things; you know that I love you."
>
> Jesus said, "Feed my sheep."[1]

In case we're not tracking, Peter fell asleep three times. Peter denied Jesus three times. Jesus hung on a cross in darkness for three hours. Jesus lay in a tomb dead for three days. And then Jesus resurrected, conquering death, sin, and failure forever.

In the first recorded conversation post-resurrection between Jesus and his disciples, he says a singular statement about peace three times. In the first recorded conversation post-resurrection between Peter and Jesus, he asks Peter a simple question *three* times.

Are you catching the significance?

Notice that Peter was hurt after Jesus asked him the third time. Why? Because Peter was still operating by the standard Jewish law of his day. If someone asks you something three times, you've reached the limit. Three questions, he's out. Point blank. Period.

But Jesus was rewriting the script.

For every abandonment, every denial, every failure that Peter had committed . . . forgiveness was waiting for him.

The New International Version translation heads this passage with the title "Jesus Reinstates Peter," because that's exactly what is happening. Peter the denier, liar, and abandoner steps fully into the namesake Jesus gave him. The rock on which Jesus will build his church. "Then [Jesus] said to him, 'Follow me!'"[2]

Wouldn't you know, this is one of the last recorded lines to Peter in the Gospels. A new story is being written. One that picks up in Acts 2 when Peter addresses the crowd with the first sermon after Pentecost. Full of the Holy Spirit, Peter the rock goes on to build Christ's church.

This is who our God is—a God who forgives. And our inability to see that doesn't change reality; it only distorts God's character in our own minds.

At your lowest low . . . you are forgiven.

God knows your intentions weren't good, but his always are.

God knows that your motives weren't pure, but his always are.

The invitation before us is to stop beating ourselves up, making excuses, and holding ourselves captive and imprisoned in shame.

Jesus Christ sacrificed everything for *you*. He gave up everything for you. He loves you. The script has been rewritten.

You are forgiven.

Prayer

Jesus,

Thank you for the gift of forgiveness.

Thank you that when I fall short, you are there to catch me.

I have made so many mistakes, yet you still love me enough to die for me.

These truths I overlook and forget remind me of my status—no longer a slave but a son or daughter.

A child of God.

This gives me confidence not to avoid your truth but to embrace it.

To ask you to help me become all you've made me to be, not in an attempt to earn anything from you—for you have already given everything to me—but to show my earnest love in response to what you've done.

May all my life be all for your glory.

Amen.

PART III

Forgiving Yourself

Day 22

SEEN, KNOWN, LOVED

There is now no condemnation for those who are in Christ Jesus.

ROMANS 8:1

The hardest person to forgive is often *ourselves*.

The pain of regret from the choices we've consciously (or unconsciously) made stings to a different degree.

Perhaps you need to hear these two truths.

1. God loves you.
2. God forgives you.

Often these truths are half-heartedly said, and the weight and power of these words are lost. But don't miss this. God *loves* you. God *forgives* you.

And he beckons you to forgive yourself, so that you can be freed to live into who he has called you to be. But the million-dollar question is *how*?

Today, I'd like to walk you through an abbreviated framework that I engage with in further depth in chapter 9 of *Three Strikes, You're Forgiven*. It goes like this:

1. DECISION

In order to get out from underneath the grip of self-hate and regret, we have to make a choice, a decision. First, to see God for who he really is. What you believe about God determines everything. A. W. Tozer said it this way: "What comes into our minds when we think about God is the most important thing about us."[1]

What comes into your mind when you think about God? Is he the God of John 3:16—the God who loves you unconditionally and with reckless abandon? Is he a God who pursues you over and over again—even when you reject him, even when you curse him, even when you deny him?

My friend, God is after you. Not in a gotcha, you're caught, shame-ridden way, but in a way that beckons and yearns for you to come out of hiding. In the loving arms of a Savior, and in the presence of brothers and sisters in the faith, you are safe.

He's there. He loves you. He sees you.

2. SUBMISSION

After we make a decision to believe God loves us and that we are forgiven, we must then enter a posture of submission.

Jesus desires for us to offer our allegiance to him because we have already been offered mercy. It's a transformational distinction, and the difference is freedom. He gave up everything; he offered up himself as a ransom so that instead of being owned by sin, shame, guilt, or regret, we can find freedom in forgiveness.

A study from the University of New York at Buffalo claims, "In order to truly forgive oneself, one must either explicitly or implicitly acknowledge that one's behavior was wrong and accept responsibility or blame for such behavior. Without these elements, self-forgiveness is irrelevant and pseudo self-forgiveness becomes likely."[2]

3. INTENTION

Once we've made a conscious decision to see God and ourselves rightly, and once we've entered into a posture of reverent submission, only then are we in a place to live out transformed intentions.

We are sinful people who fall short often. Whether we're willing to admit it or not, our intentions are not always good, pure, selfless, or kind.

But as we make the conscious decision to see God for who he really is, and as we make the deliberate choice to submit ourselves to him, he begins to redeem our lives for good.

This is a process that's often referred to as sanctification. That's what God desires for you. To become more like him. But we cannot do this if we are bound by shame and regret. Now the invitation before you and me is to forgive ourselves. To make a conscious decision to trust his character, to offer ourselves in submission to his love, mercy, and grace, and to walk intentionally in step with the God who sees, knows, and loves you just as you are.

Prayer

Lord Jesus,

Your Word says that there is no condemnation for those who are in you.

I rest confidently in that truth today.

I do not want to be bound by shame.

I want to be freed to live into who you've called me to be.

So, Jesus, as I recall the moments when I feel I have failed the most, I ask you to meet me in those spaces.

Remind me that I am not my past.

Instead, you long to restore me here—now—in the present.

I choose to believe the truth.

That you are in pursuit of me and that you love me unconditionally.

I submit my life to you. It is in your hands!

And I ask that you would transform my heart from the inside out.

That the mistakes I've made would not be repeated.

And if they are, that you would ensure grace upon grace permeates my being.

Thanks be to you.

Amen.

Day 23

FAILURE ISN'T FINAL

If anyone is in Christ, the new creation has come: The old has gone, the new is here!

2 CORINTHIANS 5:17

The top of my test had a giant "F" with a thick red circle around it.

My teacher had caught me cheating and (probably—I want to assume the best) was trying to teach me a lesson.

I have no qualms about the lesson she was trying to teach me. I was wrong for cheating on the test. But how she went about giving back my test was embarrassing.

"Here you are, Micah," she said, with no attempt to hide the giant "F" on the front page. I quickly tried to put the test away, but the damage had been done.

It was blatant. It was obvious. And the whole class could see it.

This event sparked severe test anxiety in me for years to come. The internal script that developed from that experience stuck with me. Eventually, it came to define me. No longer was I thinking, "I failed" but "I *am* a failure."

Perhaps you can relate.

The words ring and echo through your mind as they do mine . . .

When you failed your spouse and you both said hurtful words you couldn't take back.

When you failed to show up the way you wanted to for your family or friends.

When you failed to fix past mistakes and you're now dealing with the consequences.

Failure is inevitable. And yet, we've somehow convinced ourselves that failure is avoidable. That if we can avoid failure, then we can somehow self-actualize into an ideal self—that simply does not exist.

My friend, the fact of the matter is that if you're reading this, you've failed. So have I. It's inevitable. To fail is to be human. It's the starting point for all of us. And I'm not sure if you've caught on to this, but life ends in perceived "failure." We've never found a way to beat death. It wins 100 percent of the time.

But here's where the beauty of the gospel comes into play. The good news is that your failure isn't final. We serve a God who took on all your failures—past, present, future—and nailed them to a cross. Three days later, he rose, conquering death and sin forever.

This is a radical, reality-altering truth.

Your failure isn't final. Instead, you and I are extended grace and mercy to try again. And again. And again.

Please don't mishear me; never are these attempts to earn anything. We can't earn our way into heaven. We can't earn our way into love. We can't earn our way into perfection. No one can.

But the gospel offers an alternative story.

The gospel is about a God who pursues us. Who freely gave what we could never earn. Who sacrificed his one and only Son so we could be reconciled. So we could experience everlasting life.[1]

The gospel frees us from rules-oriented religion. We no longer have to walk on moral eggshells, because the same Spirit that raised Christ from the dead now lives in us.[2]

In other words, you are not the sum of your past failures.

The prophet Isaiah writes, "Forget the former things; do not dwell on the past. See, I am doing a new thing! Now it springs up; do you not perceive it? I am making a way in the wilderness and streams in the wasteland."[3]

I have found comfort and power in this truth. No longer am I defined by my failures—or my perceived failures—but I am defined by the "new thing" that the Spirit is continually doing within me.

This truth has freed me to be able to forgive. The gospel reminds me that the ground is level at the foot of the cross. We "all have sinned and fall short of the glory of God."[4]

And if failure isn't final, then that means that I am more than the mistakes I've made. Your failure no longer has to define you. Instead, freedom from that label is offered to you. But forgiveness is the entryway.

Release others for letting you down. Release yourself for not always measuring up or getting it right.

Where you've been deemed a failure, God now sees a friend. He sees someone of value, worth, and purpose. Live into that truth today.

Prayer

Triune God,

Thank you for never failing.

There have been numerous times when I have fallen short, messed up, or missed the mark.

But you never have.

And despite my imperfections, you pursue me.

You're after me.

I am undone.

Father, help me to release others for the ways they have let me down.

Help me to release myself for the mistakes I've made.

And help me to remember that when I inevitably fail again, you never do.

May I rest in your perfect love this day.

Amen.

Day 24

WHAT IF?

In their hearts humans plan their course,
but the LORD establishes their steps.

PROVERBS 16:9

My mom told me it would be my biggest regret when I turn thirty. I'm two years away from thirty (at the time of this writing), and she's proving to be right.

During high school, I reached an impasse with the two biggest passions in my life: basketball and music.

I played basketball from the time I could walk all the way through college. I also picked up a violin in the fifth grade and was classically trained for six years.

Basketball I had to work really hard at to become skilled. But playing the violin came naturally to me. Instead of dreaming of being the starting shooting guard at Duke, I began to dream of sitting first chair at Juilliard.

These two passions were beginning to take up too much time though. Something had to give. I really wanted to be a collegiate basketball player, but looking back, a lot of it was for the wrong reasons.

I wanted to justify all the time and energy I'd spent honing my craft. I wanted to justify all the ways my family invested in me, like traveling around the country to different tournaments. I wanted to prove my doubters wrong. I wanted to make my dad proud.

Violin came naturally. And I knew that I could probably go further in that career than I ever could playing basketball.

Still, I ended up choosing basketball. And if you asked me to pick up a violin now, you'd probably run the other way as soon as I started playing.

Over the years, I've thought about all the opportunities I may have missed as a result of that decision. I've never been to New York City. Could I have lived there? I made no money playing basketball (scholarships notwithstanding). Could I have made money as a violinist? I've never been to the famous music halls in the world. Could I have played there?

I'm sure most of us can recollect decisions we've made that—for one reason or another—have caused regret in our lives.

You never applied for your dream job. You never found a spouse. You never had kids. And now you're wondering . . . what if?

Friend, understand that before you ever took your first steps, God saw all of your days. And whether you've made wise or unwise decisions, God is with you.

If you're plagued by regret from the past, then you're invited to choose a new present and future. Perhaps not all at once, but maybe just one step.

Apply for the job today. Remain hopeful and open to possibilities of what *could* be. Cultivate gratitude for the stage of life you're in. Missed opportunities tend to compound the longer we stay stuck in our regret.

I believe Jesus is asking you to forgive yourself for the opportunities you missed in your life. Maybe you weren't ready. Maybe you weren't grounded enough in your faith to handle whatever opportunity you passed by. You never know how God's grace and mercy may have actually been working through your inaction then.

But then is not now. In Christ, you are free to forgive yourself and move forward confidently. Maybe I'll go pick up my violin today . . .

Prayer

Lord Jesus,

Thank you for the gift of agency and the ability to make decisions.

There are certainly some decisions or missed opportunities that I regret.

But help me not to discount your grace and mercy in that.

Perhaps the life I've always thought I've wanted is actually a life that wouldn't have been as fulfilling.

Your kindness and mercy are often too great to comprehend.

Still, help me to forgive myself for the opportunities that I have passed over.

Today is the day that you have made, and I rejoice and am glad in it.[1]

I know that I can make plans, but you determine my steps.

And so, I'm choosing to trust you in the steps ahead of me.

When I am tempted to succumb to fear, increase my faith.

When I am tempted to passively move through life, help me to actively participate in the story that you are writing.

May my missed opportunities of the past be redeemed.

Lead me to more fulfilling opportunities in the future.

Amen.

Day 25

OUT OF THE DARK

Do you not know that your bodies are temples of the Holy Spirit, who is in you, whom you have received from God? You are not your own; you were bought at a price. Therefore honor God with your bodies.

1 CORINTHIANS 6:19-20

Today, I want to transparently discuss a topic that can be difficult to talk about, and one the church often shies away from: sexual sin. It's important to address this issue head-on because of how intrinsically connected our sexuality is to our relational identity. This issue can be a stumbling block in our relationship with God and other people. And rather than sidestepping it, I think it's important to name the reality that there is something about sexual sin that feels so . . . shameful. We witness it on the first few pages of Scripture. As soon as Adam and Eve realized they were naked, they sewed fig leaves together to cover themselves.[1] To hide. In fear.[2]

Since the beginning of time, God's good design for our sexuality has been warped and distorted to a point where it's all anyone thinks about and none of what we talk about. I mean, sure, broadly speaking, our culture has no issues with talking about sex—often in degrading, misogynist, boundless ways.

But as followers of Jesus, there is an incessant propensity in us to hide, to cower, and to cover up. If I were to ask you to confess any sexual temptation or sin you are struggling with—straight up—chances are, you would be reluctant to be honest.

Why? Because something inside of us tells us that there's something off about our expression of sexuality. There's something that gnaws at us, that whispers, "This isn't the way it's supposed to be."

We know that the world's approach isn't right. And when we step outside the bounds of God's created intent, we feel the weight of shame first exposed in Eden falling all over again on our shoulders.[3]

Paul has a fascinating argument with the church in Corinth in 1 Corinthians 6. He says, "'I have the right to do anything,' you say—but not everything is beneficial. 'I have the right to do anything'—but I will not be mastered by anything. You say, 'Food for the stomach and the stomach for food, and God will destroy them both.'"[4]

Here, Paul is being a great cultural commentator. He's pulling out all of the pithy, popular statements of his time. "I have the right to do anything" was most likely a favorite slogan of the Corinthians.

This is, in our generation's terms, "You do you. My truth is my truth. Follow your heart." Statements that don't necessarily denote legality but authority over external constraints.

And Paul is using these slogans as the basis for his argument.

You say, "You do you." You say, "My truth is my truth." You say, "I have the right to do anything." But not everything is beneficial.

In other words, yes, we have agency. The beauty of God's unconditional love for us is that he offered us free will. But that free will is not to be exploited or taken advantage of. There is a sense here of right and wrong. Paul is challenging the idolatry of desire. He's saying that just because we *can* do something, doesn't mean we *should*. Somewhere along the way, we have lost the ability to see the freedom that exists in constraint.

The aim is not legalistic rules but radical love. The unashamed pursuit of holiness. This has implications for all of us, my friends.

To the married: The invitation is holiness. To fidelity and commitment. To faithfulness to one spouse, for life.

To the dating: The invitation is holiness. To realign the desires of your heart to seek God first as you wait for holy matrimony.

To the singles: The invitation is holiness. To chastity and celibacy. To submit your life to Jesus. To realign the desires of your heart toward him.

To those struggling with lust or hiding a pornography addiction: The invitation is holiness. To come into the light. To be known and get help in the form of accountability from those who care about you. To realign the desires of your heart toward Jesus.

Do you see it? Paul's invitation here is not specific, it's holistic. All who apprentice under Jesus are called to offer ourselves to the Lord. To pursue holiness in all areas of life.

The church of the future—in a day and age where desire is considered primary—is one where we submit our entire lives, including our sexuality, to King Jesus. Where our ultimate allegiance is to him.

If you've come to these pages today with a proverbial fig leaf covering, if the shroud of shame and sin has overwhelmed you, there is grace available to you! Read on and notice how God responds in Genesis.

Adam and Eve were naked and afraid (before that was a TV show) and God "made garments of skin for Adam and his wife and clothed them."[5]

My friends, these were not leaves. They were garments of skin.

Most theologians think this was the very first animal sacrifice. Because a sacrifice was a seal of a promise. The word used for these coverings is the Hebrew word *kehoneth*. We're unsure of its exact meaning, but we do know that the next time it shows up is when a young man by the name of Joseph is handed a robe—what we're told is an "ornate" or "beautiful/splendid" robe. It's a *kehoneth*. It's also the word used to describe future priest's garments.[6]

In their shame, God did not disown humanity. Instead, he clothed them in splendor and majesty to imperfectly image himself.[7]

We are offered that same invitation. To repent. To turn around. To live a different way. To come out of hiding and to receive the majestic robe of adoption that our Father has graciously given to us to inherit. There is freedom and no condemnation for those who are in Christ. We are a new creation. Live in the light of that today. Come out of the dark.

Prayer

Abba Father,

I come to you naked and unashamed.

Here I am. All of me.

Rather than hiding behind the fig leaves of shame and sin, I choose to be enveloped in the majesty of your splendor.

I confess that I have fallen short in many ways, including ways I haven't treated my body as a temple of the Holy Spirit.

And I understand that consequences come as a result of my choices.

But Jesus I am not the sum total of my past.

In you, I am redeemed.

In you, I am made whole

In you, I am loved.

Amen.

Day 26

FLIP THE SCRIPT

The tongue has the power of life and death,
and those who love it will eat its fruit.

PROVERBS 18:21

We all have scripts that embed themselves into our minds and bodies. Pastor Peter Scazzero often says, "Jesus may be in your heart, but grandpa is in your bones."[1] That is a profound truth.

We are often much more of our past than we'd like to admit.

Things that have been spoken over us, done to us, and said about us—for better or worse—stay with us. These are the "scripts" that tend to make up our internal dialogue.

In my own life, I can think of scripts that I've had to (and still must) work through. Scripts like *I must be perfect. I'm too defensive. I'm not good enough.* What about for you?

For instance, you may have been told that secrets are to be kept in the family. Or perhaps you were instructed to never show weakness, always put on a smile, never rock the boat, or to never ask for help. Each of these are scripts that we tend to latch on to that permeate every part of our lives into adulthood.

Spend some time reflecting on your internal "scripts." What words were spoken over you or said about you that you've held on to? Words that have become like a wound that heals and hurts and heals and hurts over time?

Now, think about how countercultural the teachings of Jesus are. He says to "bless those who curse you."[2]

That is an astonishing statement.

But that is the essence of forgiveness. Forgiveness transcends human brokenness because forgiveness transcends human reasoning and logic. It is fundamentally unfair. And yet, it is ultimately fulfilling.

What if we brought to mind the scripts that have been spoken over us, and what if we blessed the individuals who hurt us? What if we asked God to meet these people in their need for him?

What a radical idea! Yet, an idea teeming with healing potential.

Today, you have an opportunity to allow Jesus to flip the script(s) in your life through forgiveness.

Recognize that you are not the sum total of the scripts that you've been handed. Instead, another story is being written.

It is the Story of stories, and it says that you are

a conqueror (Romans 12:21)

chosen (Matthew 22:14)

valued (1 Peter 1:18)

loved (John 15:9)

redeemed (Psalm 107:2)

cared for (Psalm 112:7)

disciplined (Proverbs 3:11)

able to endure (James 1:3; Romans 5:3-4)

Let that be the script that you cling to today.

Prayer

Giver of Life,

There have been words spoken over me or about me that sting.

Often, I find myself living by these words.

The pressure to be perfect, to not cause conflict, to measure up, or to never fail can be overwhelming at times.

Jesus, I surrender these scripts to you.

You offer a better invitation, a lighter load, and a new identity.

Give me the strength to bless those who have hurt me.

Father, meet them in their own struggles.

Help them to unwind the scripts that have been spoken over them.

Holy Spirit, remind me that I am more than the words that have been said about me.

I am forgiven and loved by you, Lord.

Help me embrace that truth today.

Amen.

Day 27

GRIEVING WHO YOU WANTED TO BE

The LORD is close to the brokenhearted
and saves those who are crushed in spirit.

PSALM 34:18

I once heard a pastor say something like "In your twenties, the sole focus is all about ambitiously chasing who you are becoming. In your forties, it becomes far more about accepting who you have become."

Perhaps you've come to this point in our forgiveness journey and your grief stems not so much from internal scripts or past hurt but simply the direction that your life has gone.

Maybe you had dreams of becoming a PhD researcher, but then you had a kid at age twenty. Or you were excited to travel the world, but an autoimmune disease kept you grounded in your hometown. Or you thought by this point, you'd have the house with the two-car garage, a dog, and 2.5 kids, but you're still single with no prospect of love in sight.

Life has a way of beating us down and ironing us out. The longer we live, the more our life tends to follow one of two trajectories: one full of peace, integration, gratitude, and wholeness or one full of bitterness, resentment, and regret.

We either become *bitter* or *better*, as the saying goes.

Today, I invite you to grieve who you wanted to be. It's okay to give yourself permission to acknowledge what you hoped for.

You imagined life would be spent on the West Coast, but you're in the Midwest. You imagined you'd be far more successful in your career than you are. You imagined you'd be married but you're not.

Not acknowledging these realities is not maturity; it's avoidance. In order to appreciate what is, we must recognize what is not.

Forgive life for not being fair. Forgive yourself for the risks you did not take. Forgive others for the petty hurts and disagreements that have plagued you.

As you do, you can embrace reality. Sure, life may not look how you imagined it would, but it is the life you are living. And this day, an invitation exists to take one step closer toward or further away from who God has created you to be.

Prayer

Lord Jesus,

I acknowledge and lament that life has not panned out how I thought it would.

I ask for your help in forgiving life for my unmet expectations.

Help me to forgive you for the ways I feel let down.

Help me to forgive myself for the mistakes or wrong decisions I've made that have led to where I am.

The truth is, though, there is much to be grateful for.

So, now, I pause to reflect on all that I am and all that I have . . .

Father, this is the life that you have entrusted to me. Help me to make the most of it today. Bring to the surface of my soul any invitations you're asking me to step out of or into.

As I age, increase my discernment, wisdom, and prudence.

Help me to become more integrated, joyful, and whole.

Let the things that do not matter melt away. And let the real priorities of my life become crystal clear.

Life may not look how I expected, but there are many parts that are good, true, and beautiful.

Help me to live into those things.

And help me to embrace who I've become.

Amen.

Day 28

GRATITUDE

I am always with you; you hold me by my right hand. You guide me with your counsel, and afterward you will take me into glory. Whom have I in heaven but you? And earth has nothing I desire besides you.

PSALM 73:23-25

Life can feel—at times—like nothing more than a series of disappointments. I can't imagine how discouraged Moses must have felt when—after a lifetime of leading the Israelites in an exodus from Egypt and through the wilderness—he was denied entrance into the Promised Land. The very land that he had been seeking for a lifetime, he would never inherit. Waiting was met with disappointment.

Perhaps you can relate.

The job you thought you'd have by now hasn't materialized. The promotion never came. The marriage didn't work out. The diagnosis was terminal. Disappointment after disappointment.

It can be tempting to allow these frustrations to accrue and spiral into bitterness or cynicism. We may hold grudges against the people and places that have seemingly held us back or let us down.

Could there be any antidote to disappointment in this life? There is. Gratitude. The Catholic theologian Ron Rolheiser calls it "the fruit" that is borne from the hard knocks of life.[1]

When you have nothing left but God, you realize he is enough.

When you find yourself stuck in the mud of disillusionment, what if gratitude is able to pull you out?

When life's circumstances don't line up exactly how you'd want them to, what if you are invited into another way? An opportunity to choose joy?

And what if these are the ingredients to experiencing the breakthrough you've been in desperate need of for some time?

The apostle Peter writes, "Dear friends, do not be surprised at the fiery ordeal that has come on you to test you, as though something strange were happening to you. But rejoice inasmuch as you participate in the sufferings of Christ, so that you may be overjoyed when his glory is revealed."[2]

Do you see it? Joy and gratitude are the antidote to disappointment.

Today, allow gratitude to flood your thoughts. Regardless of your present circumstances, draw to mind the people, the places, or the provisions that you are grateful for.

Let gratitude win this day. That's the fruit of forgiveness at work in your life.

Prayer

Father God,

I am quick to recall the disappointments that I have experienced.

But today I'm choosing a new path.

In place of discouragement, I ask that you would flood my heart, mind, and soul with gratitude.

Jesus, as I look outside and see the birds of the air and the grass of the field that are so well taken care of and provided for, it puts into perspective just how much you care for me.

Life doesn't look how I'd envisioned it would.

But I am safe. I am secure. I am at home . . . in you.

Thank you for your provision in my life.

Thank you for the relationships that are healthy.

Thank you for redeeming and restoring me after I've failed or had others fail me.

Thank you for another day of life.

Jesus, thank you.

Amen.

Day 29

EMBRACE WHO YOU'VE BECOME

I praise you because I am fearfully and wonderfully made;
your works are wonderful, I know that full well.

PSALM 139:14

I was sitting around the campfire at the home of one of my heroes recently, soaking up the opportunity of a lifetime to glean wisdom in a personal setting with a few other faith leaders. As he was talking, he said something to the effect of "In your twenties and thirties, the driving force is ambition. Your sole focus is on who you can become. In your forties and onward, the driving force is anger. Your sole focus is on who you have become and wrestling down the disappointment of not becoming who you intended to be."[1]

I remember being struck by that. Though I'm not in my forties (or thirties, for that matter, which just means I have a lot of pain left to endure—kidding, but not really), I do pastor many people in their forties and beyond, and this resonates with the experience that I hear from them.

Often, when I meet with twenties and thirties, their focus is on what's ahead. The goals to achieve, the dreams to fulfill, the life to live.

Often, when I meet with those in their forties and beyond, the focus is on what's been missed. The regrets they have, the ways they've fallen short, the opportunities they missed out on.

There's something to be said about the human experience in navigating the lifelong arc of contentment. In a world that thrives on cynicism, we must ruthlessly fight for it.

Many people take the apostle Paul's words in Philippians 4 vastly out of context. He writes, "I can do all this through him who gives me strength."[2] This sounds like a great, motivational pep talk to get us through hard times. But what we might miss are the verses preceding this one, where Paul explains, "I am not saying this because I am in need, for I have learned to be content whatever the circumstances. I know what it is to be in need, and I know what it is to have plenty. *I have learned the secret of being content* in any and every situation, whether well fed or hungry, whether living in plenty or in want. I can do all this through him who gives me strength."[3]

Did you catch it? Paul says he has learned the *secret* of being content whatever the circumstances. Paul likens contentment to something more to be discovered than delivered.

Contentment isn't something that just comes with age. It's not a part of our next IOS system. It must be learned. It must be trained. It must be developed. It must be discovered.

My friend, perhaps you've come to today's reading filled with far more grief than joy, more hate than hope, more despair than delight.

I believe you are invited today to forgive life for not meeting your expectations. In some instances, life is unfair. In other instances, our poor decisions have led us to where we are. Still in other instances, a combination of both beat us down.

Paul is in prison as he writes these words—living under dire circumstances. And yet . . . he has learned to be content whatever the circumstances.

Psalm 139 likewise declares that you are fearfully and wonderfully made.

So what if, instead of regretfully lamenting who you did not become, you instead graciously celebrated who you are? What if, instead of seeking to escape your present circumstances, you embraced them?

Forgive life for not playing out the way that you wanted it to.

Explore the invitation God might have for you this day. As the psalmist writes, "This is the day the Lord has made; we will rejoice and be glad in it."[4]

May it be so, we pray.

Prayer

King Jesus,

I am so grateful for the fact that you are here, present and attuned to me, right now, in this very moment.

Thank you for your grace and mercy that wash afresh over me every day of my life.

Lord, I lament the ways that life has treated me unfairly.

And yet, I am here, now, for a reason.

You have forged me in the fire of life in a way that has prepared and positioned me for such a time as this.

So, Jesus, today I choose to rejoice!

For I am fearfully and wonderfully made.

Rather than succumbing to bitterness, I choose joy, gratitude, and contentment.

I am who you've made me to be.

Jesus, help me to love myself as much as you love me.

In you, I am made new.

In you, I have all that I need.

In you, the best is yet to come.

Amen.

Day 30

THE FRIENDSHIPS YOU'LL GAIN

There is a time for everything,
and a season for every activity under the heavens.

ECCLESIASTES 3:1

My family has moved eighteen times throughout the course of my life.

Moving was always difficult, but looking back, I am profoundly grateful for the many friends that I have been able to make.

Friends from preschool and middle school. Friends from basketball and orchestra. Friends from church and Instagram. Friends who are African, Asian, American, Hispanic, and French. Friends young and old.

And yet, I cannot say that I have one lifelong friend. Meaning, there is no one from my age zero year that—to my knowledge—I am still in relationship with (other than my parents, of course, no technicalities here).

All that to say, friends seem to come and go. And sure, some have stuck around far longer than others. But most have been seasonal.

Some faded naturally as life transitions happened. Others ended poorly and were cut off unexpectedly.

If you are human, then I think it's safe to assume that you have gained and lost friends. And maybe you're beating yourself up over the ones you've lost. Maybe it was your fault. Maybe it was theirs. Maybe the jury is still out.

Either way, friendships—for the most part—change over time. This can be a healthy part of life development and maturation, or it can be an unhealthy sign of an unwillingness to attach. I'll leave that to your discernment.

My intent and purpose today is to remind you to forgive the friends you've lost. Forgive the friend who moved on. Forgive the friend who left you out. Forgive the friend who chose other friends. Forgive yourself for doing these things to other friends.

The wisdom writer of Ecclesiastes, Solomon, says, "There is a time for everything, and a season for every activity under the heavens." This includes friendship.

Forgive the friends who have hurt you. Forgive yourself for the ways you've unintentionally hurt your friends. Grieve the friendships you've lost. Excitedly anticipate the friendships you'll gain.

And as you make new friends, receive them with the upmost joy and gratitude. They may be seasonal, or they may be foundational, but they are always to be loved and cherished.

Prayer

Lord,

You are somehow both Friend and Father.

You knew me before I was even in my mother's womb.

There is no friend that compares to you.

You have graciously given me friendships throughout life.

Some that were seasonal and others that have become central to my relational being.

Some that have filled me up and some that I've let down.

Some that have brought joy and some that have brought pain.

Help me to forgive the friends I have lost.

Help me to value the friends I will gain.

Jesus, thank you for being the Friend who sticks closer than a brother.

When all others fail, you still succeed.

Thank you for always being with me.

Help me to trust that you know what's best regarding the relationships in my life that are seasonal.

May it all be for your glory, Jesus.

Amen.

Day 31

A VISION FOR HEAVEN ON EARTH

Your kingdom come, your will be done, on earth as it is in heaven.

MATTHEW 6:10

In 1888, Alfred Nobel arose to a morning paper that had his obituary listed. Shocked and in utter distress, he began attempting to figure out why the public presumed him to be dead when he was very much alive. As it turns out, Alfred's brother, Ludvig, had died of a heart attack in France a few days earlier and the local newspaper had mistaken Ludvig's death for Alfred's. Sad as he was about Ludvig's death, what really upset Alfred was the obituary that was written . . . a scathing indictment of Alfred's life and career in the area of weapons of mass destruction.

The obituary labeled Alfred "the merchant of death," whose legacy was intertwined with his ability to develop new ways to "mutilate and kill" other human beings.

The error was later corrected, but not before Alfred had the unpleasant experience of reading his own premature death notice.[1]

Can you imagine waking up and reading about your own death? Can you picture the out-of-body experience it would be to read—in print—the totality of your life and legacy whittled down to a singular paragraph, for better or for worse?

See, Alfred had the unpleasant but unique experience of witnessing his life flash before his eyes. And the "dynamite king," as he was dubbed, was not pleased with what he saw.

What about you?

As you reflect on your life up to this point, what rises to the surface? How will you be remembered? Does this thought exercise elicit great joy and gratitude or overwhelming fear and regret?

You see, all of us worship.

The question is what or who do you worship? Despite his legacy of founding the Nobel Prize, Alfred Nobel built much of his life worshiping the idols of success, violence, and destruction. As followers of Jesus, we worship a Man who is the Way, the Truth, and the Life. Who claims to be the only source of life everlasting.

Every one of us has a story or stories that we believe. Ways to make sense of reality and life as we know it.

We take our cues from Jesus. And his cue is to pray a script that is radically countercultural to the world's.

Rather than pursuing power, we receive peace. Rather than pursuing wealth, we open ourselves to wonder. Rather than pursuing fame, we are content to build friendship with God and to entrust our future to him.

We pray, "Your kingdom come, your will be done, on earth as it is in heaven."

At its core, this is a prayer of submission.

This idea of submission is central to the gospel of Jesus Christ himself. Jesus' invitation—constantly—was "Whoever wants to be my disciple must deny themselves and take up their cross daily and follow me."[2]

This was an invitation into *daily* submission. Daily choosing to bear Jesus' name rather than our own. Denying ourselves and surrendering to Christ. His pronouncement of good news was "Repent, for the kingdom of heaven has come near."[3]

To repent means to turn around. To go a different direction. In essence, to give up your way of life and to submit to Jesus' way of life. This is the declaration we are given all throughout the Scriptures. Why? Because repentance precedes forgiveness.[4]

This pricks at our individualistic tendencies, doesn't it? But this is where the rubber meets the road. In the profession from Matthew 6, "Your kingdom come, your will be done, on earth as it is in heaven," we are reorienting our bodies, our hearts, our minds, and our souls around the way of Jesus. Around a different story from the set of stories that the world tells us regarding what leads to a life of flourishing.

We are effectively saying, *God, I'm sorry for my stubborn attempt at orienting life around myself. I give up trying to do it my own way. I submit to your will. I want your Kingdom to come to pass and for you to get the glory.*

This prayer is a proclamation, an annunciation that the Kingdom of Heaven is here. NOW. And the way to find your life is to lose it. To submit your agenda, your desires, your will to his.

I don't think it's an accident that the verses that follow say, "Give us this day our daily bread. And forgive us our debts, as we forgive our debtors."[5] Why? Because repentance precedes forgiveness.

But, my friends, it gets better. Not only did this Savior talk the talk, but he walked the walk. This was not lip service to appease a religious crowd. God incarnated himself. He appeared as a human being—in a body—on this earth. And he demonstrated for us what his Kingdom looks like. It looks like

good news for the poor,

freedom for the oppressed,

sight for the blind,

healing for the sick,

and salvation for the lost.[6]

It's an invitation Jesus not only gave but *lived*. And in living, he modeled the way forward for how we should live. We can partner with Jesus to usher in God's Kingdom here on earth now.

This prayer of submission is the portal to seeing God's Kingdom come to pass in our midst. And repentance is the entryway, reconciliation the signpost that points the way, leading to life everlasting.

Prayer

Our Father in heaven,

Hallowed be Your name.

Your kingdom come.

Your will be done

On earth as it is in heaven.

Give us this day our daily bread.

And forgive us our debts,

As we forgive our debtors.

And do not lead us into temptation,

But deliver us from the evil one.

For Yours is the kingdom and the power and the glory forever.[7]

Amen.

PART IV

Forgiving God

Day 32

CHOSEN

He asked Jesse, "Are these all the sons you have?"

"There is still the youngest," Jesse answered. "He is tending the sheep."

1 SAMUEL 16:11

I am six-feet-two-inches tall, and I weigh 175 pounds. The last time I measured, I had a thirty-two-inch max vertical (how high I can jump) and could bench-press 250 pounds (how much I can lift).

Relatively speaking, those are not the most impressive athletic measurements. So, it might be surprising to know that I was once a collegiate basketball player.

I could list off a whole host of accolades and accomplishments from my time on the court that would probably boost your confidence in my ability to play basketball.

But here's the problem: If you stuck me next to another man who was six-feet-eight-inches tall and weighed 250 pounds, who could jump thirty-eight-inches high and bench-press 350 pounds, and you had the choice to choose who would join your team, I have a pretty good guess who you would pick first.

What if that guy had never picked up a basketball before, though?

See, I've been uniquely equipped to play the game of basketball.

Long ago, a boy named David had been uniquely equipped to lead and to be a king—but the prophet Samuel almost missed it because Jesse bought into the idea that it was outside appearance alone that mattered.

But we serve a God who does not judge with the metrics we often do.

Still, this truth has not excluded many of us from the pain of being overlooked or underestimated. It has most likely happened to you, and it happened to David.

Samuel asked Jesse (David's father) to present his sons to see who the Lord would anoint as the next king of Israel.

Up first, Eliab. A fine physical specimen. So impressive that Samuel delights, "Surely the LORD's anointed stands here before the LORD."[1]

But the Lord was not with Eliab.

Then came Abinadab. He wasn't the choice either.

Then came Shammah. Neither was he to be the next king.

We read in 1 Samuel 16 that Jesse had seven of his sons pass before Samuel, but Samuel said to him, "The LORD has not chosen these."[2]

It becomes so dire that Samuel asks Jesse if he has any other sons. And Jesse sheepishly (no pun intended) replies, "There is still the youngest. . . . He is tending the sheep."[3]

I wonder what David must've been thinking when he was summoned. Can you imagine the embarrassment of seeing all your brothers lined up in front of a prophet, being told that each had been presented to be the next king and you were an afterthought?

This takes being forgotten to the next level.

And perhaps you can relate.

You faced rejection after rejection. You were the one passed over for that career or promotion. You were the one still single and seemingly forgotten.

The pain of that process may have left you jaded and distrustful of God's plan for your life.

But notice what David is doing both before and after he is anointed as king: tending sheep.[4]

David is this beautiful example of doing the best you can by being obedient to the last thing God has called you to. Yes, David has been anointed as king, but his time has not yet come. Therefore, he goes back to faithfully fulfilling the duty that God had set out before him prior to being named king.

Perhaps you've grown bitter toward others for not seeing your potential. Maybe you're even angry at God for seemingly overlooking you.

You wonder why God hasn't trusted you to find a spouse, or to have the job you want, or to have as much wealth, or influence, or success as you want.

But what if God will only trust you to the level that you're faithful to?

If it were up to Samuel or Jesse, David would never have been picked. Promotion was not on David's shoulders, though—it was on God's.

We ask God to use us for his glory. God asks us to be faithful.

So, bring to mind the moments you've been overlooked. And recognize that in the moments when you felt unseen, God saw you. The moment that you were rejected by others did not diminish your standing with God.

You can forgive them because they do have the last word on your potential.

My friend, there is no need to strive for the acceptance of others. Your overworking ambition stemming from the disapproval you received early on is not the summation of your identity.

Instead, new metrics are given. God told Samuel, "Do not consider his appearance or his height, for I have rejected him. The Lord does not look at the things people look at. People look at the outward appearance, but the Lord looks at the heart."[5]

Forgive those who have hurt you over the years. Recognize that God is after those who are after him. So place your ambition on the pursuit of his heart, and watch as your life begins to flourish.

Prayer

God Who Sees,

I am not my performance. My worth is not tied to the level of perceived value I add.

Rather, I am intrinsically loved because I am made in your image.

Jesus, help me to see myself the way that you see me.

For all the times that I've been overlooked, remind me that you never overlook me.

As I remember the moments when I was overlooked or rejected, allow me to take solace in the fact that I am in good company. Because in your Kingdom, the first shall be last and the last shall be first.

Help me not to be defined by these moments but by the moments that I ran to you first.

If I'm being chosen last, then I'm probably living aligned with you.

Over and over again, we witness you promote the least promotable, exalt the least exalted, and honor the least honorable.

You are the God who sees . . .

The marginalized . . .

The misfits . . .

The outcasts . . .

I may be considered last by others, but you first loved me.

Amen.

Day 33

WOUNDS TRANSFORMED

Unless I see the nail marks in his hands and put my finger where the nails were, and put my hand into his side, I will not believe.

JOHN 20:25

The Substance Abuse and Mental Health Services Administration (SAMHSA) defines trauma as "an event or circumstance resulting in: physical harm, emotional harm, and/or life-threatening harm" that "has lasting adverse effects on the individual's functioning and mental, physical, social, emotional, or spiritual well-being."[1]

Jesus' death was traumatic for his disciples mentally, emotionally, and spiritually. They had mortgaged everything on him being who he said he was. And he was gone. Just like that.

Devotion had turned into disillusionment. Life as they knew it had been forever upended.

Perhaps you can recall the day your life changed forever. You can remember the sights, sounds, and scene of your biggest failure, your deepest shame, your greatest nightmare. And you find yourself disappointed and disenchanted with a God who said he would save you but has seemingly abandoned you.

I think the disciple Thomas (or doubting Thomas as he's been infamously remembered) understood what that's like. For eight days, he lived in total darkness. A new reality had set in. A reality full of hurt, embarrassment, frustration, and resentment.

This is not the life I signed up for, I imagine Thomas thinking.

And then, "A week later [Jesus'] disciples were in the house again, and Thomas was with them. Though the doors were locked, Jesus came and stood among them and said, 'Peace be with you!' Then he said to Thomas, 'Put your finger here; see my hands. Reach out your hand and put it into my side. Stop doubting and believe.'"[2]

The question we might leave this story with is *Why did Jesus wait?*

It's the same question we're all asking in our own stories. Why hasn't Jesus shown up? Why hasn't Jesus healed me? Why hasn't Jesus initiated justice for the wrongs done to me?

The trauma of our past often keeps us in a pit of despair that slowly dismisses the possibility of healing ever taking place. But in time, the Wounded Healer reveals himself, scars intact.

He's waited for this moment. The moment when the pain of the world, the pain he endured, and the pain of your own past all coalesce. A moment of desperation when Jesus most clearly reveals himself to you.

Jesus encounters Thomas in the most personal and intimate way.

He meets Thomas's wounds with his own. And it is this encounter that changes everything for Thomas.

Thomas said to him, "My Lord and my God!"[3]

Thomas's life had been upended by the disappointment of the Savior's death and disappearance. But Thomas's life is even more upended by the encounter not of an empty tomb but of a risen Lord. This is the power that Jesus possesses. He's able to take all the pain, all the hurt, all the trauma—wherever it may be on the sliding scale of life—and not just defeat it, not just resurrect it, but *repurpose* it. According to Jesus, the wounds of this life do not disappear; they transform.

Trauma is redeemed not through avoidance or expiration but through encounter, through an alternative story that is entrusted to a loving, wise Savior in the context of relationship.

If all we believe about God is that he is a Savior who lived, died, was resurrected, and ascended, that is certainly enough to get us saved. But when we believe this alternative story is not just universal, but personal, that the invitation is extended to us to touch Jesus' wounds and see for ourselves that he really is who he says he is, that's what gets us healed.

Your trauma is true. Your pain is real. It should be handled with great care.

Also, Jesus really did die on a cross. He really was buried. And he really did rise from the grave. He offers us the chance to not just believe that he is Lord but to encounter him for ourselves.

The scars of your past do not disqualify you from experiencing forgiveness and reconciliation. The scars of your past are the evidence that your wounds have been healed by Jesus, singularly empowering you to extend and experience forgiveness and reconciliation in an upside-down, backward, Kingdom sort-of way.

Oh, what good news this is.

Prayer

God of Comfort,

I can't begin to explain the confusion and doubt I have experienced.

The nights I've wondered if you hear me.

The hurt that has taken place in my life is not okay. And I know you know that.

Perhaps the most difficult part of unanswered prayer is how it has affected my relationship with you.

I want to begin healing.

I want to fight back against the nagging sense of disillusionment.

I want to overcome.

You are a God who was wounded yourself.

You experienced trauma on the cross, as you had your hands and feet nailed to a tree. You were mocked and ridiculed.

You know what I've been through.

And you offer to me a way forward. A way where my struggles are not just overcome or resurrected but repurposed for good.

So, Jesus, meet me in the messes of my life.

Bring justice to my situation.

Help me to forgive you for the times I felt alone and enable me to see that you never left my side.

Redeem me, heal me, and let forgiving shalom reign.

Amen.

Day 34

THE BIG QUESTION

About three in the afternoon Jesus cried out in a loud voice, "Eli, Eli, lema sabachthani?" (which means "My God, my God, why have you forsaken me?").

MATTHEW 27:46

Can a God who allows suffering be trusted?

That's the big question, isn't it?

Often, in times of desperation, need, or fear, we turn to God and await a miraculous rescue.

Isn't that what God is supposed to do?

God is love. God is perfection. God is whole. And he loves *us*, right?

So how do we forgive him when it feels like he's absent? Silent? Nowhere to be found?

It feels right to pin any sort of pain on a seemingly pain-free God.

If God is all-powerful, why doesn't he step into my situation? If God is all-knowing, why doesn't he stop the evil before it comes? If God is all-present, why doesn't he make himself known to me?

These are all good, difficult questions that followers of Jesus have been asking for millennia. In fact, these questions are not evidence of doubt, but of *faith*. It takes faith to examine our beliefs and ask God our honest questions about suffering.

How, then, are we to reconcile with a God who has seemingly let us down? How do we forgive God?[1] We begin by looking to God himself . . .

God the Son had prayers that went unanswered. God the Son felt abandoned by God the Father. God the Son endured God the Father's silence and seeming absence.

How about Jesus' prayer in the garden of Gethsemane on the eve of his crucifixion? "My Father, if it is possible, may this cup be taken from me."[2] In other words, "Father, if I don't have to die, please don't make me." That prayer went unanswered.

Or how about Jesus on the cross? "About three in the afternoon Jesus cried out in a loud voice, '*Eli, Eli, lema sabachthani?*' (which means 'My God, my God, why have you forsaken me?')."[3]

This is God asking God, "Where are you?"

And there's . . . silence.

My point in sharing all of this is that our propensity to argue that God is merely someone who "doesn't understand" or "is aloof" or "doesn't care" seems to not hold its weight.

We are talking about a God who "gave his one and only Son"[4] to die so that you and I could live. A God who at some level has experienced unanswered prayer, rejection, silence, abandonment . . . and yet was able to faithfully declare, "Yet not as I will, but as you will."[5]

As we learn the art of forgiveness, we will find ourselves developing more and more gratitude for all that God has done, is doing, and will do.

So, as we attempt to reconcile with God, let's enter in with a posture of humility, recognizing that we are talking to and about Someone who understands—with holes in his hands as proof.

And let gratitude spring forth from the struggle.

Prayer

God of the Universe,

I can't pretend to understand all the intricacies and complexities you hold together moment by moment.

But I lament the seeming gaps and holes that exist in my life.

The ways that people have failed me or I've failed them.

The struggles that have come my way.

It all feels unfair.

And yet . . .

You are a God who experienced it all yourself.

You endured suffering, silence, and rejection.

Your faith, hope, and love remained.

So, even though I do not understand, you do.

Even though I am not in control, you are.

And when I do not know how to express what I am feeling, Holy Spirit, speak for me with wordless groans.

Help me to forgive the things that I do not understand.

And meet me in my honesty. Remind me that you are near.

Amen.

Day 35

THE (DAILY) CHOICE BEFORE YOU

Whoever wants to be my disciple must deny themselves and take up their cross daily and follow me.

LUKE 9:23

Forgiveness is a practice. It's a conscious decision. It's a decision we have to make routinely. We must choose to leave our sin, put it to death, and to go another way. This is what's referred to as repentance.

The same pattern applies to the process of forgiveness. We must choose to hate the sin of what has been done to us (seek justice), choose forgiveness (love mercy), and proceed in submission to the Lord (walk humbly).[1]

Forgiveness is the decision God made two thousand years ago, once and for all time through the shedding of his Son's blood on a cross. Jesus put to death the sin of all humanity—past, present, and future. As Jesus himself said, "This is my blood of the covenant, which is poured out for many for the forgiveness of sins."[2] This act was the culmination of a plan that was put in motion the moment Adam and Eve fatefully chose sin over union with God.

From that day on, what began with the question "Where are you?" led to God's unceasing pursuit of you that culminated in the blood of Jesus Christ.[3]

In other words, though Jesus' sacrifice is for all time, the outworking of that sacrifice occurs *daily*. Look at the prayer structure Jesus models for us: "Give us *today* our daily bread."[4] And the very next line? "Forgive us our debts, as we also have forgiven our debtors."[5] We can assume that Jesus wants us to pray for forgiveness at the same rate that we pray for food (daily).

Many of us fall into the trap of subconsciously believing that God loves us because Jesus died for us. Right? We might think, *God has to forgive me because I put my faith and trust in Jesus. He doesn't actually want to.*

We see God the Father as this ruler of the cosmos who's separate, jaded, and upset with humanity because we can never get it right or figure it out. *Thank goodness for Jesus, because if it weren't for Jesus, God would hate us.*

Does this way of thinking resonate with you?

Here's the deal: God does not love us because Jesus died for us; Jesus died for us because God loves us. Such a subtle shift, but one that will change your perspective forever.

Read John 3:16 through *that* lens! "For God so loved the world . . ."

He—God—so loved the world—that he gave (or he sent, or he offered) his one and only Son, that whoever believes in him shall not perish but have eternal life.

See, God the Son is the fulfillment of eternal reconciliation, while God the Father is the orchestrator of it. God the Father is the originator, the genesis of reconciliation.

So, we daily pray for forgiveness, as we also have forgiven our debtors.

In other words, we are instructed to ask for forgiveness and to extend forgiveness daily.

My friend, you may be feeling frustrated while reading this because you thought you forgave what that person did to you years ago by putting it behind you. But forgiveness doesn't mean forgetfulness. And often, forgiveness is not a one-stop shop.

Usually, forgiveness is a journey. A journey of daily asking for and receiving grace.

Release yourself from the burden of needing to be at a certain point in the process. Instead, make a conscious decision today to forgive, trusting in the Lord's strength to empower you.

And then tomorrow, do so again.

And again.

And again . . .

Prayer

Lord Jesus,

There are certain parts of my story that I can't seem to shake.

I feel like I should be past them, over them, moved on from them.

But here I am. Stuck.

I'm wondering if that may not be a bad thing.

Instead, perhaps it's just being human.

Your sacrifice on the cross forgave all my sins—past, present, and future.

But the outworking of that forgiveness is a daily experience.

Help me to practice what you mercifully offer me: daily bread. Daily forgiveness.

Jesus, this day, I offer to you only what I can.

Would you remind me that is enough?

In your grace and mercy, I choose forgiveness today, tomorrow, and the next day.

Amen.

Day 36

COVERED BY GRACE

The very hairs of your head are all numbered. Don't be afraid; you are worth more than many sparrows.

LUKE 12:7

I find it both comforting and discouraging that God knows every hair on my head.

On the one hand, how could he not? He is God. He is the Lord of the universe.

On the other hand, his omniscience means that he knows all of my future mistakes before I make them. The perfectionist in me sees land mines ahead that I desperately want to avoid. Legalism calls my name in an effort to ensnare me into a works-based life that I think will keep God happy with me so long as I do not mess up.

On occasion, this has caused me great fear—not in reverence toward God but in apprehension toward failure. The hypotheticals play over and over again in my mind.

God knows what's coming. And yet . . .

> While we were still sinners, Christ died for us.
>
> **ROMANS 5:8**
>
> Neither death nor life, nor angels nor rulers, nor things present nor things to come, nor powers, nor height nor depth, nor anything else in all creation, will be able to separate us from the love of God in Christ Jesus our Lord.
>
> **ROMANS 8:38-39, ESV**
>
> We should be called children of God.
>
> **1 JOHN 3:1**
>
> I have loved you with an everlasting love; therefore I have continued my faithfulness to you.
>
> **JEREMIAH 31:3, ESV**
>
> Out of his fullness we have all received grace in place of grace already given.
>
> **JOHN 1:16**

Now, this is not to deter us from growing and maturing into the image of Christ. It is actually to spur us on. We are not under the pressure of a scorecard, needing to achieve the perfect record in order to win. My friend, the game has already been won.

You are forgiven.

For the regrets of your past.

For the mistakes of your present.

And for the failures in your future.

God's grace covers it all.

The God who knows all, knows all. And still, he chose you. He loves you. He forgives you.

So, live into that grace, and let him lead you to life everlasting.

Prayer

God of grace,

You know the hairs on my head, the thoughts in my head, and the ways I'm in over my head.

And yet, you still love me.

Oh, Father, help that truth to sink in.

As far as the east is from the west, so you have removed my sins.

What good news this is!

In you, I am a new creation.

So, Jesus, help me to live into who you've called me to be.

When I inevitably fail, fall short, and sin, lead me back to the cross.

Remind me that I am safe in your arms.

May the old country of sin grow further and further in my rearview mirror, and let my eyes be fixed on the road of righteousness ahead.

You see the mistakes I'll make; help me to receive the grace that's offered.

Amen.

Day 37

A VISION FOR SINGLES

I wish that all of you were as I am.

1 CORINTHIANS 7:7

For almost a year, Taylor would come over regularly to participate in the Sabbath with Rylei and me. We would talk about the exciting things happening in her life, her travels, what God was stirring in her soul, and of course, we would watch Marvel movies.

That season helped reframe the beauty of singleness for me. Here was a young woman who was single and content. Who was learning to live within the limits of the present season of her life and who was thriving as she pressed into the particular freedoms afforded to her.

If you're single, the church and I owe you an apology. Somewhere along the way, we lost the plot of the Scriptures and determined that singleness was second-rate. We decided that it was marriage or bust as a follower of Jesus and that those who did not find a spouse were somehow defective, lost, or less-than.

But this is not the case.

Jesus, for one, was single. Paul too. Paul has some fairly strong language in 1 Corinthians 7 concerning the beauty of singleness and the benefits it offers. He says, "I wish that all of you were as I am," and to the unmarried and widows he says, "It is good for them to stay unmarried, as I do."[1] Paul wasn't someone who believed singleness is somehow second class.

Maybe, like Paul, you are content in your singleness. That is wonderful! Singleness can be a gift when chosen and embraced!

Or maybe you long to find a spouse.

To those of you who are single and ready to mingle, perhaps you're working through the frustrations of a desire that has (up to this point) been unmet. An invitation exists for God to meet you in your longing.

Maybe you need to forgive him for not agreeing to align his will with your timeline. Rather than living in bitterness because of who you're not doing life with, what if you were able to reframe the unique freedoms that inherently exist in singleness? I know this is an intensely personal subject for many of us. But please hear me, my intention is not to diminish the real ache that you may experience. Instead, my heart is to help you break free from any bitterness your present reality may—unknowingly—be holding over you. And to gently challenge you to consider whether there's more to be embraced in this present season of your life.

God longs to meet us in our good desires, but he also recognizes that what we hope for may not always be what we need. And, in my experience, it is our true desires that he is consistently seeking to coax out.

My friend Christine has been single most of her adult life and is one of the sweetest, most peaceful, Jesus-like people that I know. Her willingness to embrace singleness and find contentment—even as she wrestles in the tension of her longings—has spoken volumes to the character that Christ is forming within her. This is not to say that God couldn't have done the same work had she been married, but her story has allowed her to uniquely witness to others who find themselves on a similar journey.

So, to the singles—like Christine—perhaps you need to work through the frustration you feel with the ways the church and its people have treated your singleness. Maybe you were looked over, passed up, or left out. Perhaps you were always prodded for updates on your next "prospect," and it felt as if no one wanted to actually get to know *you*. Maybe you've stayed single long enough for people to distance themselves from you, confusing your singleness with some sort of stunted maturation. These are all things that unfortunately I've had to process with single friends throughout my time as a pastor. And it's not fair. So, I'm sorry. Please forgive the church for the ways that we have discredited you.

And now, live into the vision of your life that God has for you. Certainly, bring the desires of your heart ever before him, but learn to embrace who is in front of you. The world needs you, as you are. As Paul concludes, "Each person should live as a believer in whatever situation the Lord has assigned to them, just as God has called them."[2]

As you are called, you are enough.

Prayer

Jesus,

You are the Lover of my life.

In a Christian culture that has consistently acted intolerant of my single status, you see me.

In fact, you know—intimately—what it is like to live like me.

You were single and satisfied, living life to the full.

So, God, help me to embrace such a vision for my own life if you've called me to singleness.

I offer my longings to you.

I forgive you for the ways you've seemingly been absent, distant, or silent.

I trust the deeper work that you are doing within me right now.

And I ask that you help me to embrace a vision for a life of fulfillment in whatever situation you assign to me.

Amen.

Day 38

A HAVEN FOR THE BROKEN

"Never will I leave you; never will I forsake you."

HEBREWS 13:5

How do we forgive the church? How do we forgive the place that was supposed to keep us safe, welcome us in, and offer us a home to belong when it does the exact opposite?

Leading a church of my own nowadays, I so love and value the community of people that I do life alongside. Still, I sometimes incur hurt from "the church"—my own congregation!

I've experienced the full gamut of people being people.

I've been cussed out on the phone by a raging parent for attempting to hold their daughter accountable. I've had leaders enthusiastically sign up to lead and serve, only to abandon ship soon after. I've been gaslit, strung along, and outright denied opportunity by leaders ahead of me.

I've witnessed double standards and hypocrisy at different levels of organizational leadership. I've watched countless coworkers be sidelined, shamed, and silenced under the guise of protection of the broader institution. I've had numerous conversations with individuals who have left church leadership, the church itself, or following Jesus altogether because of painful past experiences.

In light of this, a question I am often asked is how I'm not jaded toward God or the church. You'd think that after enduring multiple massive church scandals, it'd be easy to blame the church.

And there have certainly been seasons when I have.

God, how could you?

God, why?

God, make this right!

I've prayed Psalm 109 countless times in fits of righteous anger toward some of the appalling, cowardly acts I've seen done "in the name of the Lord." It grieves my heart to no end.

But over time I've come to a place of trust and hope in the Lord. I can't blame the church, because I've seen God—time and time again—use what Satan meant for evil, for good. I've seen beauty come from ashes. I've seen restoration take place. I've seen wrongs made right. Every time, it is a glimpse of heaven.

Those experiences don't make past hurts any less painful or wrong. But God's faithfulness, mercy, and kindness shine brightest in the darkest spaces.

In the suffering of church hurt, I have found, over and over, a God who sees me. Who cares for me. And who cares for his church. We mustn't forget this, my friends. It is God's church. Our job is to be faithful to the calling of building his church, but he is the one who makes it happen. This is good news, because even when we fail, God does not.

I have found no other avenue to bring healing, hope, and restoration on earth as it is in heaven than the local church. Our church here in Indy is not perfect by any stretch of the imagination, but we've made it our ambition to become, in part, a haven for broken people. That piece of our mission statement was born out of deep pain in my past. But it's a past I wouldn't trade for the world, because God has redeemed it, forgiven it, and restored my present. My future is secure in him. I take heart in the words of God from the writer of Hebrews: "Never will I leave you; never will I forsake you."[1]

Forgiveness is possible when we realize that we're not in control of the church. God is. The local church is worth fighting for. It's worth belonging to. And so, if you find yourself in a season of church hurt, please take time to heal. But do your part to heal. Let Jesus' words of wisdom, compassion, and love act like a healing balm to your soul.

And then return. Try again. Root yourself in a community. You will risk being hurt. And you probably will be hurt again. Failure is inevitable. But belonging, community, family is just on the other side. When it goes right, it's but a taste of what is to come.

Prayer

Lord,

I have been let down by your people, the church.

There have been things said about me, done to me, and spoken over me that have caused pain in my life.

Where do I go with this, Father, other than to you?

I know you can handle it.

And I know it pains you too.

This is not the way you intended it to be.

Yet, as imperfect as it is, the vehicle you have used to bring the hope of Jesus to the world is the local church.

So, I covenant myself.

As Ruth said to Naomi, "Your people will be my people and your God my God."[2]

This is my attitude toward the church, Jesus.

Despite what I have experienced, I will not give up.

I will not give in.

Bitterness has no hold on me.

Instead, I will get up and try again, trusting that the faithful are out there, ready to be found.

And when I do find the community, family, and belonging that I've been looking for, remind me that it—too—will not be perfect.

More struggles will come.

But you are the Wounded Healer, transforming me into your very image.

So, wounds, come.

Healing will be here soon after.

Heaven on earth can be experienced here and now, now and not yet.

Amen.

Day 39

A VISION FOR HEALING

Do not take revenge, my dear friends, but leave room for God's wrath, for it is written: "It is mine to avenge; I will repay," says the Lord.

ROMANS 12:19

Many of us are in need of healing. Others of us have been struggling to forgive. Pain may be trapped so deep within that we feel like we've had something permanently taken from us.

If you have been hurt in this way, I am so, so sorry. Understand that as we envision a way forward of forgiveness, you are not being asked to excuse or deny what took place. Forgiveness is not forgetfulness.

The temptation many of us face when we've been hurt is threefold. Either we . . .

1. Deny—we stuff down the hurt and pretend the offense never took place, allowing time to substitute for healing.
2. Offer conditional forgiveness—we attempt to "play God" and take over the situation in an effort to protect and shield ourselves from future pain.

3. Hold on to an offense—we live out the old adage "an eye for an eye," believing that if we've been wronged, then we are justified to equally wrong someone back.[1]

Each of these tendencies comes back to the root of control. It is easier for us to control, mitigate, and manage the pain than to release it to Jesus for healing.

There is but one way to freedom in your future, my friend. And it is through forgiveness.

Forgiveness becomes a message to either accept or reject. Jesus has empowered and authorized us—as his followers—to declare the good news of his forgiveness. Why? Because he first forgave us. It is not ours to withhold or rescind. He alone is the judge of the world. We are the messenger; he is the message.

> If you forgive other people when they sin against you, your heavenly Father will also forgive you. But if you do not forgive others their sins, your Father will not forgive your sins.
>
> **MATTHEW 6:14-15**

> Do not judge, and you will not be judged. Do not condemn, and you will not be condemned. Forgive, and you will be forgiven.
>
> **LUKE 6:37**

> When you stand praying, if you hold anything against anyone, forgive them, so that your Father in heaven may forgive you your sins.
>
> **MARK 11:25**

> Watch yourselves. If your brother or sister sins against you, rebuke them; and if they repent, forgive them. Even if they sin against you seven times in a day and seven times come back to you saying "I repent," you *must* forgive them.
>
> **LUKE 17:3-4, EMPHASIS MINE**

> Peter came to Jesus and asked, "Lord, how many times shall I forgive my brother or sister who sins against me? Up to seven times?" Jesus answered, "I tell you, not seven times, but seventy-seven times."
>
> **MATTHEW 18:21-22**

To clarify, this good news of repentance, forgiveness, reconciliation, and restoration is for everyone; no ifs, ands, or buts about it.

"Well, that's not fair!"

"You don't understand what was done to me."

"You don't know what happened."

I don't disagree with you. However, Jesus does: "If you do not forgive others their sins, your Father will not forgive your sins."

This is one of the most explicit statements on forgiveness that Jesus offers throughout all the Gospels, and it is *scandalous*.

I wish there was a way to dismiss, deny, or explain away this teaching. It certainly would justify the internal bitterness and strife we hold on to, wouldn't it?

But Jesus is clear: Unforgiveness leads to unforgiveness. There's truly only one way forward. The spiritual writer Henri Nouwen said it this way: "By not forgiving, I chain myself to a desire to get even, thereby losing my freedom. A forgiven person forgives. This is what we proclaim when we pray, 'and forgive us our trespasses as we forgive those who have trespassed against us.' This lifelong struggle lies at the heart of the Christian life."[2]

The apostle Paul writes, "Do not take revenge, my dear friends, but leave room for God's wrath, for it is written: 'It is mine to avenge; I will repay,' says the Lord."[3]

Jesus is inviting you and me to trust him. It is not on us to avenge the ways we've been hurt. A day is coming when all wrongs will be made right. When all of us will give an account.

Until then, we press on, living and becoming wounded healers, like the one we were made to reflect: "He was pierced for our transgressions, he was crushed for our iniquities; the punishment that brought us peace was on him, and by his wounds we are healed."[4]

Healing is within reach—and it looks like the nail-scarred hands and feet of Jesus.

Prayer

Jehovah-Rapha,

You are the Lord, our healer.

I must admit that there are parts of me that don't want to follow your instructions for forgiveness.

There is an incessant desire within me to fight back.

But as I step back, I think about the unintended consequences that line of thinking has.

For whatever I do to others, so would be done to me.

I am not exempt from the human condition.

I have failed and fallen short.

I have made mistakes.

So, Jesus, forgive me.

And knowing that I am forgiven, instill in me the strength to forgive others.

Remind me that you are the one who will make all things right.

Justice is yours alone.

Amen.

Day 40

THE GOD WHO FORGIVES YOU

While he was still a long way off, his father saw him and was filled with compassion for him; he ran to his son, threw his arms around him and kissed him.

LUKE 15:20

Rembrandt was a seventeenth-century Dutch painter, and he created one of my all-time favorite paintings: *The Return of the Prodigal Son*. It sits in my study, and I look at it every morning. If you're unfamiliar with that story, here's a brief synopsis.

In Luke 15, Jesus tells a parable about a man who has two sons. The younger son asks for his share of the estate, effectively wishing his father dead. This was an insult of the highest form and extremely disrespectful. Surprisingly, the father allows the request of the younger son.

So the younger son takes off and squanders his inheritance in wild living. A famine hits the land, and the younger son becomes so desperate for survival that he becomes a farmhand and finds himself longing for the pods he's feeding to the pigs. It is at this moment that the young man comes to his senses and concocts a plan to return home and to beg his father for mercy. To not even reestablish his sonship but to take on the nature of a servant.

The young son returns home, but before he can get to his father, his father *runs* to him (an extremely embarrassing practice for an ancient Middle Eastern man), throws his arms around him, and kisses him.[1] The son sheepishly tries to get his pathetic apology out, but the father has none of it. He has the servants bring a robe and ring to the son, kills the fattened calf, and throws a feast for the son who was lost and is found.

It's a beautiful, beautiful story.

But I want you to observe how Rembrandt portrays the father figure (God). Looking at a picture of the painting online, what do you notice?

Do you notice that the father is blind? That he does not *see* the physical mess, the uncleanliness, the raggedness of his wayward son?

Do you notice the father's hands? His left hand is a masculine hand—pulling the son in as a loving, safe father, reminding the son that he is secure in his father's arms. His right hand is a feminine hand—consoling the son, reminding him that he is in tender, loving care.

Do you notice the father's facial expression? It is neither disgusted nor disappointed. There's grief for the pain his son has endured, relief that the son has returned, but overall, a calm, collected *presence*.

Love made known.

But the story doesn't end there. Because in Rembrandt's painting, we also see on the right side a man looking down in contempt. This is the older brother, whom Jesus describes in detail.

> Meanwhile, the older son was in the field. When he came near the house, he heard music and dancing. So he called one of the servants and asked him what was going on. "Your brother has come," he replied, "and your father has killed the fattened calf because he has him back safe and sound."
>
> The older brother became angry and refused to go in. So his father went out and pleaded with him. But he answered his father, "Look! All these years I've been slaving for you and never disobeyed your orders. Yet you never gave me even a young goat so I could celebrate with my friends. But when this son of yours who has squandered your property with prostitutes comes home, you kill the fattened calf for him!"
>
> "My son," the father said, "you are always with me, and everything I have is yours. But we had to celebrate and be glad, because this brother of yours was dead and is alive again; he was lost and is found."
>
> **LUKE 15:25-32**

Perhaps, as we conclude our journey together, there is still someone you're holding bitterness and resentment toward. You just can't seem to understand how God could ever forgive them for what they've done.

My friend, may I gently encourage you—as the father did—to fix your gaze. To not focus on what they get but on what you get. "Everything I have is yours," says the father.

Complicated relationships, difficult environments, mismanaged resources, and misaccusations are distinctive marks of life here on earth. And yet, we follow a God who endured all of that and then some. Who still had the strength to declare, "Father, forgive them, for they do not know what they are doing" even as he was nailed to the cross, naked and exposed and ashamed for all to see.[2]

How in the world could you forgive _____? You fill in the blank . . .

My honest answer?

How could we not?

Each and every day, I find myself messing up, falling short, and missing the mark. I am a wretched sinner, saved by grace. As Paul says, "All have sinned and fall short of the glory of God."[3]

We have come to the end of our journey of forgiveness. And perhaps there is a piece of you that still doubts God could ever forgive you for the things that you've done. But to believe that is to misunderstand the God we serve. He is a God of mercy. A God of forgiveness. A God of reconciliation. A God of love.

God is love.[4]

You who have gone wayward, God beckons you to return. He will restore who you were made to be. He is asking you to repent—to turn around from the way you've been going and to come home.

He's waiting for you. And as soon as you're in view, he's running toward you with a ring and robe, ready to embrace you as the son (or daughter) that you are.

The telos—the end goal, the aim—all throughout Scripture is clear. Love.

And the journey toward that end—all throughout Scripture—is clear. It is forgiveness.

In appendix A, I have compiled about seventy verses from Genesis to Revelation that address the topic of forgiveness. This is not an additive but a central component to the Story of stories that is being written. At the end of days, "He will wipe away every tear from their eyes, and death shall be no more, neither shall there be mourning, nor crying, nor pain anymore, for the former things have passed away."[5]

All the hurt, pain, death, and destruction of this world will melt away. And what will be left will be the reconciled heaven and earth, with God and on the throne of his everlasting Kingdom.

That is good news, my friends.

The lost will be found.

The dead will become alive.

Celebration and joy will permeate.

Everything I have is yours.

Rejoice.

Forgiveness will not fail.

Prayer

Father,

You are a God of forgiveness.

Thank you that when I run away, you keep watch for me.

Thank you that when I return, you run toward me.

Thank you that when I return, you greet me with a warm embrace.

I am so undeserving of your mercy. And yet, in your kindness, you welcome me home.

Jesus, I know this is but a foretaste of what is to come.

Eternal forgiveness, healing, and reconciliation await me in the age to come.

Until then, may I be a vessel of forgiveness toward my neighbor and myself. May my hope in the restoration and redemption of your blood be evidence that a new way of life is possible.

I close this journey of forgiveness with the only words that can suffice . . .

"Thank you, Jesus."

Amen.

Epilogue

WHAT IS TO COME—A TABLE WHERE ALL ARE WELCOME

On the third Friday of every month, I leave straight from my early morning workout, visit my wife at her chiropractic office, and then—sleepy and sweaty—pull into the parking lot of the Yolk restaurant nearest my house. It's 7:30 a.m., and I sip my glass of water and scan the menu (even though I already know what I'm going to get—two eggs, scrambled). Right on time, Jake and Matt stroll in.

They sit down and we begin our monthly rhythm of confession. Jake starts by explaining some of the issues he's internally wrestling with. Matt shares about some insecurities he's been feeling. I go last and share about my impatient attitude with Rylei and my overall tendency to work too long and ignore my family.

We get it all out on the table. The good, the bad, and the ugly of our souls. The resentment we're holding on to, the pain of our past, the mistakes in our relationships. We give each other space to be heard, and we listen intently. If a follow-up question needs to be asked, we ask it. If accountability needs to be instituted, we offer it. Over the years, we've added a practice at the end of our time together where we say to one another, "You are seen. You are loved. You are forgiven."

These are healing words.

These are restorative words.

These are words that center me back into my identity in Christ.

It forces us to—if there is any bitterness or resentment we're holding on to toward each other—release the hurt.

It forces us to—if there is any regret, guilt, or shame we're holding on to toward ourselves—let go.

It's become one of my favorite spaces—around the table.

During Jesus' earthly ministry, we see him reclining "at the table" while interacting with common people and sinners as he furthered his Kingdom work. This is also where true community and genuine fellowship among his disciples developed.[1]

The early church gathered regularly in homes, around the table, to "break bread together" as a practical expression of their fellowship in Christ.[2] The apostles also exhort us to show hospitality.[3] Finally, God's Word declares that eating together is important through the apostle John's depiction of the great marriage supper of the Lamb, which says,

> Then I heard what sounded like a great multitude, like the roar of rushing waters and like loud peals of thunder, shouting: "Hallelujah! For our Lord God Almighty reigns. Let us rejoice and be glad and give him glory! For the wedding of the Lamb has come, and his bride has made herself ready. Fine linen, bright and clean, was given her to wear."

> (Fine linen stands for the righteous acts of God's holy people.) Then the angel said to me, "Write this: Blessed are those who are invited to the wedding supper of the Lamb!" And he added, "These are the true words of God."
>
> **REVELATION 19:6-9**

My friends, the Story is going somewhere. In the age to come, we will spend our days not in white robes, endlessly singing a hymn on repeat. No, we will work, play, eat, drink, and laugh together. Joyous, soul-quenching eternal communion with God and our brothers and sisters in Christ is detailed through the sharing of a meal at the wedding supper of the Lamb.

And my friends, this table will include all who have accepted Jesus as Lord and Savior. I think we will be much surprised to see who is sitting there when all is said and done.

As followers of Jesus, reconciliation must always be our ultimate desire. A forgiving future must be our aim. Reconciliation is central to our story because it is the crux of God's story. He is a forgiving God. Reconciliation is at the very core of the gospel—the good news—of Jesus. It is what distinguishes us—in part—as followers of Jesus. We are to be Christ's ambassadors of his reconciliation to the world.

God will one day return to reclaim and reconcile all of creation. What was once deemed the greatest failure imaginable (Christ's death) led to the greatest victory (the resurrection), and his return will be the most triumphant redemption of all time. When it's our turn to step onto the stand, what will our defense be? We've already been proclaimed guilty . . . But wait. Jesus steps up to take our place. God is finding us—not guilty. Whatever sins you've been holding on to, whatever hurt you've experienced, it's already forgiven and made right. Our failing present is not the end of the story. Remember? God has not forgotten you.

Our forgiven future is already secure.

Healing is possible. On the other side is the life you've always longed for. A life of freedom, a life of peace, and a life of love, around a table.

The poet John Shea is attributed as saying, "The heavenly table—the banquet table—is open to everyone who's willing to sit down with everyone."[4] As the Catholic theologian Ronald Rolheiser comments, "[If] I'm not willing to sit down with everybody, it's not God who's excluding me. . . . [If] everybody in heaven [is] angry at each other, we've got earth."[5]

My friend, the Story is going somewhere. And it includes a table in the presence of our enemies, our friends, our family, our coworkers, strangers, refugees, and more. Indescribably, there's a seat at this table for you and me too.

The question is, who are you going to invite to it? The reality is, the table I share with Jake and Matt has been formed and fashioned over years of meals, fights, and laughs. Like any covenant relationship, you can't know until you've experienced it. But here—five years into these friendships—I offer to you a vision of the immense beauty of a relationship where one can be deeply known and loved. And I hope you are beginning to desire the same, a taste of what we all will one day be invited into.

There can be few best practices or easy applications. You must simply begin, wherever you are, today. Begin cultivating the table that is to come. A table where confession, forgiveness, and reconciliation have the final say. A table where heaven touches earth.

A table with Jesus at the head and the center.

Forgiveness forever and ever.

Amen.

THANKS

This book was born out of a teaching reflecting on pain. A few hours later, Sarah A. at Tyndale told me *that* teaching was the basis for my next book. I never thought I'd ever be asked to write on a topic as weighty as forgiveness (and a devotional at that!), but I'm grateful to Sarah for believing that I had this in me all those years ago.

Claire Lloyd—for catching the vision for this and fighting for what's necessary.

Dan Balow—I still can't believe you took a chance on a twenty-five-year-old kid. To see where we've come . . .

Kara Leonino, Stephanie Abrassart, and the entire Tyndale Team—you guys make this process so incredibly fun.

Sibyl and Dick Towner and The Springs staff—spiritual direction, walks in the labyrinth, prayer in the chapel . . . I cherish all of it. See you next month.

The Sanctuary—it's hard to put into words how much has changed in just a few years. What was once a dream is now a reality. And it is so much sweeter than I ever could have dared imagine. Until Indianapolis looks like heaven . . .

Jake Hirsch—y'know, for basically everything.

The Sanctuary's staff and board—for championing my unique calling as a pastor/writer, writer/pastor and empowering me to live into this.

The Brotherhood—Tom, Slav, Nick, Caleb, Aaron, Jenson. The company of pastors inspiring me in so many ways. Onward.

CC—we've had to live much of this out the last few years. Thanks for being the relational crucible that's given weight and shape to these words.

Walsh's—for the sacred space and slow days, oh and an author picture that my wife *really* likes.

Lij, Zay, J&J—I'm for you, always.

Mom and Dad—for staying together, doing the hard work, and modeling forgiveness and reconciliation over and over . . . and over again.

Ry—for choosing me even when I fall short. Your love teaches me so much about Jesus'. I love you. Forever and ever.

Writing a book is a laborious, time-consuming, pedantic process. It goes in starts and stops, over years, distilling ideas into actual words on pages. This would not be possible without the help of so many of the people mentioned above and others that I missed.

Overall, I am just so, so grateful.

Appendix A

VERSES ON FORGIVENESS

I have found that on particular days being able to locate what God's Word says about forgiveness is extremely helpful and comforting. And so, I've taken time to compile what the Bible has to say regarding forgiveness in the order that the verses occur canonically. I hope and pray they bring peace and hope to your soul in times of need.

Genesis 50:17
Exodus 10:17
Exodus 23:21
Exodus 32:32
Exodus 34:9
Numbers 14:19
1 Samuel 15:25
1 Kings 8:30
1 Kings 8:50
2 Chronicles 6:21
2 Chronicles 7:14
Psalm 19:12
Psalm 25:11
Psalm 32:5
Psalm 65:3
Psalm 79:9
Psalm 86:5
Psalm 103:10-14
Psalm 130:4
Proverbs 28:13

Isaiah 1:18
Isaiah 53:5
Isaiah 55:7
Jeremiah 5:7
Jeremiah 31:34
Jeremiah 33:8
Jeremiah 50:20
Daniel 9:19
Hosea 14:2
Micah 7:18-19
Matthew 5:23-24
Matthew 6:9-15
Matthew 18:15-18
Matthew 18:21-22
Matthew 18:35
Matthew 26:28
Mark 2:10
Mark 11:25
Luke 5:24
Luke 6:37
Luke 11:4
Luke 17:3-4
Luke 19:8
Luke 23:34
John 17:20-23
John 20:23
Acts 2:38
Acts 3:19
Acts 5:31
Acts 10:43
Romans 8:1
Romans 12:18
Romans 12:14, 15-17, 19
2 Corinthians 2:5-11
2 Corinthians 5:18, 20
Ephesians 1:7
Ephesians 4:31-32
Colossians 1:13-14
Colossians 3:13
2 Timothy 3:1-5
Hebrews 8:12
Hebrews 10:17
Hebrews 12:14-15
1 Peter 2:21
1 Peter 2:23
1 John 1:9
1 John 2:1
1 John 2:3, 6, 9-10

Appendix B

THE BACKPACK

It was filled to the top
And my back was aching.
Therefore I had to stop,
Good friendships I wasn't making.

As I walked through life
I just couldn't keep going.
So I stopped by the roadside,
My pack was overflowing.

It was really full of books,
I was surprised what was there.
But I had picked them up,
I certainly don't know where!

On the top was Bitterness and Anger,
Next was An Unforgiving Spirit.
The next book was How to Get Even.
To forgive, I wouldn't hear of it!

On the bottom I found my Bible,
God's Word I'm glad I could find,
Praying for wisdom to lighten my load,
I needed contentment and peace of mind.

I found verses on forgiveness and love,
The Holy Spirit brought peace from above.
Jesus died and arose to eliminate strife,
To improve relationships in our life.

Please forgive those who hurt you,
Then God will forgive your sin too.
You just hurt yourself if you don't forgive.
Read God's Word, in obedience live.

Now my backpack is pretty light,
I try to carry things that are right.
Why hold a grudge, life goes so fast.
God's Word declares that love will last!

MARTY WALSH[1]

NOTES

PROLOGUE: PROCEED WITH CAUTION

1. Ron Rolheiser, "Getting It Down to the Essentials," Ron Rolheiser, June 27, 2010, https://ronrolheiser.com/getting-it-down-to-the-essentials/.
2. Blake Gopnik, "'Golden Seams: The Japanese Art of Mending Ceramics' at Freer," *Washington Post*, March 3, 2009, https://www.washingtonpost.com/wp-dyn/content/article/2009/03/02/AR2009030202723.html.
3. Tiffany Ayuda, "How the Japanese Art of Kintsugi Can Help You Deal with Stressful Situations," NBC News, updated April 28, 2018, https://www.nbcnews.com/better/health/how-japanese-art-technique-kintsugi-can-help-you-be-more-ncna866471.

DAY 2: TRAINING WHEELS

1. John Mark Comer, Practicing the Way, Church Formation Incubator, October 5, 2023.

DAY 3: SIBLING RIVALRY

1. Genesis 4:3-4.

DAY 4: CALLED BY NAME

1. Todd W. Hall with M. Elizabeth Lewis Hall, *Relational Spirituality: A Psychological-Theological Paradigm for Transformation* (InterVarsity Press, 2021), 6.

DAY 5: THE PLACE OF HONOR

1. Mark 10:42-44.

DAY 6: KILL KEYBOARDS WITH KINDNESS

1. 1 Kings 18.
2. 1 Kings 19:2.
3. 1 Kings 19:3.

4. Ephesians 6:12.
5. James 3:4-5.
6. 1 Peter 3:9.

DAY 7: BEGINNING THE PROCESS

1. For those unfamiliar with my family's story, you can read about it in my parents' memoir: *Beyond Ordinary*. I don't unpack much of it in this book, as it's their story to tell, not mine.
2. "Facts About Divorce in America 2024," *Terry and Roberts* (blog), May 6, 2024, https://terryandrobertslaw.com/blog/divorce-rate-facts/.

DAY 10: IN HIS HANDS

1. Daniel Hitz, "The Power of the Mother Wound," Reconciliation Ministries, August 28, 2018, https://recmin.org/newsletter-1/2018/8/28/the-power-of-the-mother-wound.
2. Isaiah 49:16.
3. Deuteronomy 32:11.
4. Matthew 23:37.

DAY 11: FORGIVING AND LETTING GO

1. To clarify, I do believe the Scriptures are clear that infidelity (and abuse) are the only clear grounds for divorce (Matthew 19:8-9). Restoration and reconciliation should absolutely be pursued if possible. However, if any other issues in a marriage arise, they should be worked through thoroughly and with supreme commitment to holding the marriage intact. Divorce—no matter the circumstances—is never the primary option for human flourishing.
2. 1 Corinthians 5:5.
3. From my mentor, Steve Carter.

DAY 13: SPEAK LIFE

1. Genesis 27:19, emphasis mine.
2. Laban lies about offering Rachel to Jacob as a wife and deceptively offers Leah (Genesis 29:25), Rachel lies about stealing her father's idols (Genesis 31:34-35), Joseph's brothers lie to Jacob (Genesis 37:31-32), etc.
3. Christian B. Miller, "Are Most People Liars?," *Forbes*, October 17, 2022, https://www.forbes.com/sites/christianmiller/2022/10/17/are-most-people-liars/?sh=2683acd9bd58.
4. Proverbs 10:11.

DAY 14: CONFESSION

1. Matthew 15:22.
2. Luke 17:13.
3. Matthew 20:30.
4. Psalm 51:17.
5. 1 John 1:9, NKJV.

DAY 15: ASK

1. Romans 8:1-2.
2. Blue Letter Bible, "metanoeō (*v.*)," accessed November 7, 2024, https://www.blueletterbible.org/lexicon/g3340/kjv/tr/0-1/.
3. Romans 7:15.

DAY 16: COME INTO THE LIGHT

1. Matthew 6:23.
2. Psalm 147:5.
3. John 3:21.
4. Psalm 30:5.

DAY 17: A NEW MARRIAGE

1. Because of this oath, Jesus has become the guarantor of a better covenant (Hebrews 7:22).
2. 1 John 4:8-12.
3. 1 John 1:9.
4. Deuteronomy 31:6-8.

DAY 18: FALLING FORWARD

1. Romans 3:23-24.

DAY 19: A VISION FOR COUPLES

1. Ephesians 5:21.
2. Ephesians 5:33.
3. Ephesians 4:26.

DAY 20: NOT TOO LATE

1. Genesis 37:18, 28.
2. Genesis 45:5.

3. Desiring God CEO Marshall Segal talks more about this in this article: "You Can Forgive Your Parents," Desiring God, February 8, 2017, https://www.desiringgod.org/articles/you-can-forgive-your-parents.
4. Ephesians 4:32.
5. 2 Corinthians 5:17.
6. An indirect quote from Segal, "You Can Forgive Your Parents."

DAY 21: REWRITING THE SCRIPT

1. John 21:15-17.
2. John 21:19.

DAY 22: SEEN, KNOWN, LOVED

1. Justin Taylor, "Tozer vs. Lewis: What's the Most Important Thing About Us?," The Gospel Coalition, June 4, 2016, https://www.thegospelcoalition.org/blogs/justin-taylor/tozer-vs-lewis-whats-the-most-important-thing-about-us/.
2. Julie H. Hall and Frank D. Fincham, "Self-Forgiveness: The Stepchild of Forgiveness Research," *Journal of Social and Clinical Psychology* 24, no. 5 (2005): 626, https://fincham.info/papers/Self-Forgiveness-jscp-in%20press.pdf.

DAY 23: FAILURE ISN'T FINAL

1. John 3:16.
2. Romans 8:11.
3. Isaiah 43:18-19.
4. Romans 3:23.

DAY 24: WHAT IF?

1. Psalm 118:24.

DAY 25: OUT OF THE DARK

1. Genesis 3:7.
2. Genesis 3:10.
3. I want to take a moment to acknowledge that you may be experiencing shame that was never meant to be yours to carry. If that is you, I am so sorry. Know that God sees you, and this was never part of his design. The burden of someone else's sin is not your shame—it is theirs. If you feel safe, reach out to someone you trust such as a pastor or Christian counselor who can begin to help you work toward healing.

4. 1 Corinthians 6:12-13.
5. Genesis 3:21.
6. Blaine Eldredge, *The Paradise King: The Tragic History and Spectacular Future of Everything According to Jesus of Nazareth* (Iona Farms Books, 2023), 40–41.
7. Psalm 104.

DAY 26: FLIP THE SCRIPT

1. Pete Scazzero (@petescazzero), "Jesus may be in your heart, but grandpa is in your bones," Twitter (now X), June 30, 2017, https://x.com/petescazzero/status/880864831808700416.
2. Luke 6:28.

DAY 28: GRATITUDE

1. Ron Rolheiser, "Getting It Down to the Essentials," Ron Rolheiser, June 27, 2010, https://ronrolheiser.com/getting-it-down-to-the-essentials/.
2. 1 Peter 4:12-13.

DAY 29: EMBRACE WHO YOU'VE BECOME

1. John Mark Comer, Practicing the Way, Church Formation Incubator, June 13, 2024.
2. Philippians 4:13.
3. Philippians 4:11-13, emphasis mine.
4. Psalm 118:24, NKJV.

DAY 31: A VISION FOR HEAVEN ON EARTH

1. Evan Andrews, "Did a Premature Obituary Inspire the Nobel Prize?," History, updated July 23, 2020, https://www.history.com/news/did-a-premature-obituary-inspire-the-nobel-prize.
2. Luke 9:23.
3. Matthew 4:17.
4. 2 Chronicles 7:14; Luke 17:3; Acts 2:38; 1 John 1:9.
5. Matthew 6:11-12, NKJV.
6. Luke 4:18-19.
7. Matthew 6:9-15, NKJV.

DAY 32: CHOSEN

1. 1 Samuel 16:6.

2. 1 Samuel 16:10.
3. 1 Samuel 16:11.
4. 1 Samuel 16:11, 19.
5. 1 Samuel 16:7.

DAY 33: WOUNDS TRANSFORMED

1. "Trauma and Violence," SAMHSA, last updated November 8, 2024, https://www.samhsa.gov/trauma-violence.
2. John 20:26-27.
3. John 20:28.

DAY 34: THE BIG QUESTION

1. Let me add that from a theological perspective, God does not need our forgiveness. His ways are perfect. He is perfect. But from a relational perspective, it is difficult for us to love someone we do not trust. Forgiveness—I've found—is the pathway to learning to trust God, especially when his ways do not align with my ways.
2. Matthew 26:39.
3. Matthew 27:46.
4. John 3:16.
5. Matthew 26:39.

DAY 35: THE (DAILY) CHOICE BEFORE YOU

1. Micah 6:8.
2. Matthew 26:28.
3. Genesis 3:9.
4. Matthew 6:11, emphasis mine.
5. Matthew 6:12.

DAY 37: A VISION FOR SINGLES

1. 1 Corinthians 7:7-8.
2. 1 Corinthians 7:17.

DAY 38: A HAVEN FOR THE BROKEN

1. Hebrews 13:5, which is actually a quote from Deuteronomy 31:6.
2. Ruth 1:16.

DAY 39: A VISION FOR HEALING

1. Loosely adapted from this article from Parkway Church, "Forgiving Someone Who Hurt You Deeply," *The Parkway Church* (blog), accessed March 6, 2025, https://www.theparkwaychurch.com/blog/forgiving-someone-who-hurt-you-deeply.
2. Henri J. M. Nouwen, *The Road to Daybreak: A Spiritual Journey* (Image Books, 1990), 68.
3. Romans 12:19.
4. Isaiah 53:5.

DAY 40: THE GOD WHO FORGIVES YOU

1. Matthew Williams, "The Prodigal Son's Father Shouldn't Have Run!: Putting Luke 15:11-32 in Context," *Biola Magazine*, May 31, 2010, https://www.biola.edu/blogs/biola-magazine/2010/the-prodigal-sons-father-shouldnt-have-run.
2. Luke 23:34.
3. Romans 3:23.
4. 1 John 4:16.
5. Revelation 21:4, ESV.

EPILOGUE: WHAT IS TO COME—A TABLE WHERE ALL ARE WELCOME

1. Luke 5:29; 7:36; 11:37; 14:15.
2. Acts 2:40-46.
3. Romans 12:13; Hebrews 13:2; 1 Peter 4:9.
4. Ronald Rolheiser, interview by John Mark Comer, posted October 4, 2023, Practicing the Way, Vimeo, https://vimeo.com/871265124/0c9d2d7867.
5. Rolheiser, interview by John Mark Comer.

APPENDIX B

1. "The Backpack" has been reproduced with permission from the author.

ABOUT

HEY THERE!

A bit about me . . .

I live and write inside "the loop" of Indianapolis, Indiana, with my wife, Rylei, and our Australian kelpie, Leo.

I'm the pastor of teaching and vision at The Sanctuary.

I'm the author of *Trailblazers: A Journey to Discover God's Purpose for Your Life*.

I believe that the written and spoken word are mediums to elicit heart change and life transformation. I've committed my life to using words for *good*.

Thanks for joining me on this journey. I hope and pray this work has blessed you in some way.

WHAT NEXT?

Good books deserve to be shared.

If you've found this work helpful, it would mean the world to me if you'd consider

- posting a review at your favorite online bookseller;
- posting a picture on social media about why you enjoyed the book;
- sending a note to a friend who you think would benefit from this work. Or, even better, gifting them a copy yourself.

After a good read, I'm always looking for more. If it's helpful to you, below is a QR code to access more of my teachings and writings on faith, formation, and the life of Jesus.

You can also learn more at sanctuaryindy.com or by visiting micahedavis.com.

May the peace of Christ be upon you,